Pr‍

The Hitler Years Through the Eyes of a Child

No academic lessons or battlefield tours could have prepared me for this incredible, coming-of-age memoir of wartime Germany as experienced by one girl, Charlotte. Her story is unique in expressing the emotion and knowledge of those years as she takes us through unexpected moments of humor and levity woven into her chilling memories of WWII. Charlotte gives voice to those seldom heard, and puts my experiences with the veterans of The Great War into a more personal perspective. *The Hitler Years Through the Eyes of a Child* reminds us that some people truly are made of stronger stuff—strength, resilience, honesty, and integrity. Charlotte is one of them. This is not a story of Hitler and WWII, it is the story of two people, Charlotte and her mother, who helped change the course of history one life at a time.

— Fred Nace is a retired Military Intelligence Officer with peace-keeping and combat tours throughout Europe and Southwest Asia.

Speaking as a professional defense analyst of World War II for forty years, I strongly endorse this excellent book and recommend that it be read widely. Written in a lucid style that is both passionate and insightful, Charlotte Self's memoir provides a masterful and fascinating account of how life unfolded for average German citizens during the long nightmare of Hitler's rule, his tyranny over the entire country, and his aggressions in World War II. More important, it provides deeply probing insights into the hearts and souls of the many honorable Germans who hated Hitler and tried to avoid serving him.

This dark period in Germany's history and the destruction it experienced should never be forgotten. The war was a disaster for Germany, and the suffering of average Germans was staggering. Even so, Hitler was unable to extinguish the decency of many Germans. This is precisely why West Germany, after the war, quickly emerged as a stable democracy and a good ally of the United States and its NATO partners.

Because Charlotte's inspiring memoir casts a bright spotlight on good Germans and their opposition to Hitler, it deserves to be read as a seminal contribution to the vast literature on Nazi Germany and World War II in Europe.

— Dr. Richard L. Kugler holds a PhD from MIT and is an expert on European security affairs having worked at the Pentagon, RAND, and the National Defense University. He is author of twenty books on Europe and global affairs.

Charlotte's captivating book relives the wisdom and bravery of her physician mother and grandmother who bravely and wisely shielded their charge from Nazi indoctrination.

The child Charlotte had matriculated to young adulthood before fully grasping the enormous gravity of the Holocaust that had consumed her native land. But as time passed, she matured and developed her thinking to become more aware of and aghast at the horrors that had been inflicted on her fellow Germans.

She carried those painful memories deep in her soul, and had all but buried them in her memory bank, until she finally unearthed them in a dramatic and poignant fashion. She had to dig painfully into her historical recollections and perspectives in order to memorialize them accurately and interestingly, and she paid the price to do both. The result is this splendid book.

Having been a refugee once and an immigrant three times, Charlotte expresses great sympathy for those who must take flight to escape persecution, or worse; and admiration for her native Germany, which in 2015 opened the door to more than one million people that would otherwise be homeless.

Charlotte often says: "Love and kindness restored me, and that is why I feel so strongly that every refugee deserves to find open arms . . . somewhere."

Jack J. Prather is the author of Six Notable Women of North Carolina *and* Twelve Notables of Western North Carolina.

The Hitler Years Through the Eyes of a Child

2nd Edition

The Hitler Years
Through the Eyes of a Child

2nd Edition

Charlotte Hugues Self

ISBN-10: 0-9978961-5-9
ISBN-13: 978-0-9978961-5-2

Library of Congress Control Number: 2017951752

Cover design by Chris Alexakis

Published by The Cheerful Word
224 Thompson St. #259
Hendersonville, NC 28792-2806

Order additional copies at www.Amazon.com

Dedication

This book is dedicated to my mother, Dr. med. Anne Marie Hugues, whose wholehearted devotion to all humanity has been an inspiration to me throughout my life.

Contents

✦

Prologue

As I sit in the new chapel of the Kaiser Wilhelm Memorial Church in Berlin, the tinted light of the huge blue glass window embraces me. This chapel is a place of meditation and reflection for me, where the whispered voices and shuffling feet of tourists and visitors have a strangely calming effect. I enjoy a wonderful feeling that I am not alone.

I close my eyes, awaiting the inner peace and serenity for which I came, and there it is again: the nightmare of my childhood, which has haunted me my whole, long life.

Without warning or invitation, I once again hear the goose-stepping of those black, polished boots and the raucous, brawling voices singing about the *Vaterland* and how they are going to put the whole world at their feet. There are endless rows of men dressed in black and khaki brown, pounding and making those awful, discordant noises that I can still feel after all these years.

Then, just as I cannot stand it any longer and am ready to get up and run out of the church, the mighty church bells begin to ring, loud and powerful, and the building is filled and vibrating with their magnificent sound, overcoming the ugly memory with a strength and peace.

The pounding feet and guttural songs are silenced and finally, finally, in the all-embracing ringing of those bells, the nightmares of eighty years, along with the horror and the fear, drift away and become a memory.

Yes, just a faded memory.

From East Prussia to Mecklenburg

Even after all this time I remember that sunny day in September of 1931, just after my fifth birthday, as if it were yesterday.

My mother and I got on a train in Ortelsburg in East Prussia where we lived, and as it slowly pulled out of the station I thought it was so strange that my father was not standing on the platform waving goodbye. When I looked up at my mother, I saw that she was looking out of the window as if she could not see anything. Two tears were slowly running down her face. As I reached up to touch them I asked, "*Mutti*, will we ever come back?"

Without moving her head or her eyes, she whispered, "No, never ever again."

That startled me, and I caught my breath. For a moment I did not know what to do or what to say, so I curled up beside my mother, put my head in her lap, and let the gentle rocking of the train calm me down.

Bumpety bump, *niemals wieder*, never again.

Bumpety bump, niemals wieder, never again.

I did not go to sleep, but I was not awake either, because I could not feel the pain.

Niemals wieder, never again, bumpety bump.

My thoughts drifted back to that day at our tiny cabin in the forest at the Masurian Lakes. I saw myself standing for hours in the shallow water with a fishing pole, hoping that no fish would bite because I would not have known what to do, since killing one was not an option.

As I was standing there in the utter stillness which I so loved, a huge silver cigar appeared from behind the trees, drifted across the sky, and disappeared on the other side as silently as it had come. I kept that as my secret until a few days later, when somebody brought a newspaper into the house and my mother called out, "Look here, *Löttcken*, Graf Zeppelin has flown over East Prussia, and they took a picture of it."

You should have seen the expression on their faces when I quietly said, "Yes, I know; I saw it."

My mother and I had stayed at that little house every summer for as long as I could remember, and I loved it because I felt completely free. There were so many berries and mushrooms to pick. I built fences of long pine needles to keep in the frogs and beetles. No luck there. The beetles would just scuttle away, but the frogs would destroy my fences as they just ran through them instead of elegantly jumping over them, which I hoped they would do.

Every two or three days a farmer would come, deliver the mail and a newspaper, and take us into the village of Passenheim. We would do some shopping, but mostly we went there so that my doctor mother could make house calls on every patient in the neighborhood. She never charged a penny, and that had made the two of us an honored part of the community.

After a while on the train I asked my mother, "Mutti, where are we going?" and she answered the two wonderful words, "To *Oma*." That was better than saying, "Straight to Heaven!"

My grandmother had been our only visitor at our cabin, and I adored her. She had raised five children, her patience was endless, and she taught you things and praised you when you got it right. There was nothing I would not have done for my grandmother for as long as she lived.

Many years later I learned that my grandmother had never wanted to visit us in Ortelsburg. My father was there, and my grandmother could not bear the idea that he would not permit my mother to practice medicine. "A woman's place is in the home!" he proclaimed.

And that was why we were on our way to Mecklenburg now.

Bumpety bump. *Wir gehen zu Oma*. We are going to Oma. Bumpety bump.

After my mother and I had returned from our last trip to Passenheim, I noticed that there was a strange tension in the house. I never heard any arguments between her and my father, but there were a lot of calm discussions with Fräulein, our housekeeper, whose name I never knew.

I felt lonely and excluded since nobody would tell me what was wrong. I saw my father so seldom that I was always on my best behavior, and I, the chatterbox, really did not know how to talk to him. Eventually, a lot of large suitcases and an overseas trunk came out and were packed, and shortly after my fifth birthday, at the end of September 1931, Mutti and I were on that train.

The train went all the way from Ortelsburg, via Danzig, to Mecklenburg. All the doors were locked as we passed through the "Corridor." At the end of the First World War at the Treaty of Versailles, that German piece of land, stretching from Silesia to the Baltic with the important seaport of Danzig, was given to Poland, and it separated Germany from German East Prussia.

I cannot remember how long we were on the train, but it was a very long time and we may even have changed trains. I have no idea how the transfer of all that luggage was accomplished, but as the train pulled into the station in Rostock, Mecklenburg, and I saw my tall, elegant grandmother standing on the platform, waving a huge scarf high in the air, I knew all was well and I never looked back.

My grandmother lived in Schwerin but had a fisherman's cottage in Wustrow auf Fischland in Mecklenburg. My mother had to change trains in order to go on to Schwerin, and it had not been clear to me that I would stay with my grandmother at her cottage.

We saw my mother off to her platform, and as she and grand-mother embraced to say goodbye, I heard my mother whisper, "Take care of her; she has an eating problem."

That was the first I had heard about that, and I decided to ignore the statement, just as I had ignored several whispered words during the last few weeks.

We helped my mother onto her train with her luggage—some porters had taken care of the huge overseas trunk—and as the train pulled out of the station, I snuggled into my grandmother's big skirt and waved. But I was so glad to be with Oma that I forgot to cry.

Amber and Chalk

It would have been a long walk from the Wustrow train station to my grandmother's little fisherman's cottage, but she had asked a local fisherman to meet us at the station with his horse and wagon, so we rode home in style. I had never met a fisherman before because I had never been near the sea, and the fisherman was intrigued that I did not know that not everyone who lived in the country was necessarily a farmer. He explained that hardly anything would grow in the sand dunes of the Baltic, but the fishing was great and a man could make a very good living.

I ought to have been very tired after that long train ride, but as soon as we arrived at the thatched cottage, I jumped off the wagon and ran into the garden.

What I remember most are the flowers. The garden seemed huge to me—a giant field of flowers with little paths in between and one large apple tree with endless numbers of tiny, green, in edible apples in the middle. I don't remember any berry bushes or other fruit trees.

Behind the apple tree was an outhouse, which I immediately explored, and I saw to my great delight that there was a toilet I could use all by myself. It was a wooden bench with a hole and a lid, and there was actually a roll of toilet paper and not bits of newspaper on a nail, as I had seen in the farmers' outhouses in East Prussia.

As you walked into the house you came through a big Dutch door, and I remember that the upper part of that interesting door was closed only during very bad weather and at night. From there you entered a huge room, which must have been a barn at one time. There was a big stove in one corner with pans hanging all around it, a table, and a sink. Over the sink was a pump, and that was the only place where you could get water in the entire house. I thought that was great. I did not like to get washed, and I never drank water anyway.

The rooms were small, with low ceilings and tiny windows that did not let in much light. There were many lamps, all with hand-made shades and silk flowers, and the pictures on the walls were also mostly of flowers, hand-painted by my grandmother. Every room was indescribably colorful and cozy.

I don't remember my mother's goodbye or my eating problem or where I slept, but I do remember the next morning. Oma made me a cup of cocoa and sliced up an apple, and when I did not touch either and just kept walking around the house, she quietly put everything away, took me by the hand and said, "We are going to the beach."

"Beach?" I asked.

In all my five years, I had never heard of such a thing. It was quite a long walk through the village and then through green meadows, and all of a sudden, there it was! Beyond a white strip of sand there was an endless expanse of gently moving water. Never in my life had I been anywhere where my eyes could see as far as they could see. I tiptoed to the edge, letting the gentle water play over my hands, and asked, "Can I go in?"

Oma said, "Of course." She took off my dress, shoes, and socks and just let me go.

I was fearless. I ran into the water, jumped up with every gentle wave, and came back to the beach only when I had really had enough. When the sun had dried my little body, Oma slipped my dress over my head and said, "Now we must look for amber."

Eighty-five years ago, the Baltic beaches were quite different from the polluted strips of sand that lie there now. They were practically untouched by human beings and had not been robbed by endless numbers of tourists, campers and, yes, even refugees. The ancient treasures of the sea were there for the taking.

We collected lots of seashells, which delighted me greatly. Then Oma picked up a little yellow, transparent rock, but when she put it in my hand, I found that it was not like a rock at all. It was so light that I could not feel the weight of it on my hand. I asked if I could keep it and was so pleased when Oma said, "Of course."

Oma suggested that we look for some chalk, and again I asked, "Chalk? What's that?"

"You find it on the beach, and you write with it on a slate," she said.

What a learning experience, as I did not know about either chalk or a slate. So we looked around, and Oma found a white rock about an inch in diameter, which she put in my hand. It was not as light as the amber but was much lighter than a stone.

On the way home we stopped in the little schoolhouse, and Oma managed to talk the teacher out of a writing slate for me. That night I had my first writing lesson, writing with the chalk from the Baltic Sea, on a proper school slate, by the light of one of the oil lamps with a beautiful shade covered in silk flowers. By bedtime I could print the word MUTTI, the German word for mommy.

There was still the issue of my eating problem. Several times during the day Oma would ask me, "Are you hungry?" and I would answer, "No," and run out into the garden. Sometime during the afternoon, Oma called from her Dutch kitchen door—I remember this as clearly as if it had happened yesterday—and I came running.

On the ledge of the door was a small wooden board—the kind people use in Northern Europe to this day when they eat sandwiches—and on it was a thick slice of heavy German rye bread, spread with a thick layer of country butter. Oma just held out that piece of bread and, quite naturally to me, I took a big bite and ran off again. Oma stood quietly behind that kitchen door. And, yes, I did come running by to take another bite, running around the apple tree, around the flowerbeds, and around the outhouse, always returning for another bite until the bread was gone.

Nothing was ever said about eating, but every day in the early afternoon Oma stood in the kitchen door with a thick slice of bread, to which a big mug of sweetened buttermilk was later added. After four or five days of that loving, understanding care, my eating problem was gone—for life.

I do not know how long I was with Oma, but it must have been three or four weeks. When my mother came back, I ran into her arms. I remember shouting, "I can write, and I can eat!" My mother hugged me tightly; I can just imagine the glances she and Oma exchanged.

It was wonderful having my mother there. I took her to the beach and showed her how to look for amber and chalk and proudly demonstrated the letters and numbers I could write on my slate with that wonderful piece of chalk from the Baltic Sea.

My grandmother's bedroom was really just a curtained-off partition of the living room, and while Mutti was there she slept on the daybed in the bedroom and I was bundled up in a huge down blanket on the living room sofa. I remember the dim light and the muffled voices of my two favorite women in all my life. They could not see me, on my knees behind the curtain, seeing their outlines and listening to every word they were saying.

They were planning just how they would arrange Oma's house and their lives to make all of our lives a success. I heard things like, "She can sleep in my bedroom; you can set up a bed in the loft so she will not be disturbed when you go out at night, and the patients can wait in my living room." And on and on.

As I think back on those nights, I wonder why I was not disturbed by all of that whispered planning, but I was not, not for a minute. If it was planned by Oma or Mutti—and especially by both of them—it was bound to be okay. That sense of security in the presence of either my mother or my grandmother has stayed with me all my life, even though my mother has been dead for thirty years and my grandmother for over sixty. Just thinking about them or looking at their pictures makes me feel warm, secure, and loved.

By the end of September the three of us were on the way to our new home in Schwerin, a beautiful little town in Mecklenburg, and I was ready for a new adventure.

Schwerin: Capital of Mecklenburg

To give you a picture of how and where we were going to live, I have to describe what once was, and forever will be, my hometown.

Surrounded by seven lakes and seven forests right in the middle of one of the most fertile areas of Europe, Schwerin—the capital of Mecklenburg, which had 52,000 inhabitants—was really still a feudal city. The *Großherzog* (archduke) was in his castle, a beautiful building reminiscent of the castles in the Loire region of France.

The upper class lived in the lovely parts of the town and were pretty much clustered together beyond the castle gardens and park. I don't know how many people belonged to that class, maybe 10 percent of the population. They were the gentry, those whose names started with "von." Also living there were high-ranking officers originally in the service to the *Kaiser*, as well as some bank directors, doctors, and lawyers. But the professional people belonged in this class only if they came from proper families.

Social order is very important in small towns all over Europe, even to this day. The only thing different from town to town and from country to country is the basis for this elitism. In Schwerin you could not buy into that set, you could not educate yourself into it, and you even had a hard time marrying into it. You either were or were not part of the elite class by virtue of your birth alone. It so happened that my mother was part of this elite class—and that she was so active in following her social democratic principles and was a divorced, female doctor does not seem to have hurt her at all.

There was no industry around Schwerin; in fact, there was hardly any in the whole of Mecklenburg. But it was a rich agricultural region and, together with Pommern (Pomerania), the land next door, was often referred to as the breadbasket of Germany. There existed no abject poverty, and there were no slums.

I have to admit, Mecklenburg was well behind the times, probably by about fifty years. Some Westerners and some Bavarians claim this to be true even to this day, and that may be so. Now, I may be misquoting, but I have heard that Konrad Adenauer is supposed to have said, "When it is time for me to die, I'll just move to Mecklenburg; that way I am going to live for another fifty years."

All this is probably a bit of an exaggeration, but in the 1930s Mecklenburg was certainly no breeding ground for National Socialism or the violence that that system was to bring. The people were content, they had recovered from the inflation of the 1920s, things were slowly getting better, and they had never particularly cared about the "shame of Versailles."

We took the streetcar, a new experience for me, from the station to Bismarck *Platz* and walked up a hill to Oma's house. I had one hand in Oma's and the other one in Mutti's, and safely between the two of them I skipped confidently into a new life.

Living with My Grandmother

Oma's house seemed huge with three stories and a basement, a bay window on every floor, a balcony, and a small yard with lots of flowers and a birdbath. There was also a tiny garden house and a place to hang the laundry to dry. What I did not know until years later was that my grandparents had lost all of their considerable fortune in the Great Inflation of 1923. The Treaty of Versailles had imposed a huge war debt on Germany, and the government—the Weimar Republic—kept printing worthless money until a loaf of bread cost two billion marks. After my grandfather's death in 1927, my grandmother subdivided her beautiful three-story house into apartments, which she rented to either two or three families.

I shall never forget, for as long as I live, the first time I saw my grandmother's living room. I stopped dead in the doorway and let my eyes roll around the room. My brown eyes were exceptionally large for such a small person, and I loved rolling them around, squinting and doing other eyeball tricks. I once even held my squint for the entire duration of a clock striking twelve. Nothing happened, in spite of my grandmother's repeated warnings that my eyes would stay that way if I made that face long enough.

Anyway, I let my eyes slowly take in the entire room, feeling as if I were entering an enormous, mysterious, and somewhat overwhelming place.

On the left was a huge, white-tiled, almost floor-to-ceiling stove. Nothing too exciting there; I had seen those before, just not quite as gigantic as that one. Then came a wall with maybe ten or twelve oil portraits—different shapes and sizes, all mounted in gold frames. Later, I was to learn that those were my ancestors and that each and every one of them had a story, which I heard as the years went by.

In front of those portraits was some fancy furniture—Biedermeier, I was later told. All of the chairs had beautifully colorful seats, and the sofa had lovely large pillows with flowers—tapestry, as I learned it was called—and some were even done in tiny, intricate Gobelin stitching.

The real eye-catcher was a grand piano, standing right in the middle of that immense room. It was grander than I could have ever imagined, with an intriguing, lacy green piano cover. The word Steinway was painted in gold letters above the ivory keyboard.

The large, round dining room table had an embroidered table-cloth, and on the far right wall was a floor-to-ceiling china cabinet. Everywhere stood lamps: big ones and small ones, on the piano, on every sideboard, and in the center of the living room and dining room tables. I could not count, and I do not remember, how many lamps there were, but I found out later that my grandmother hated the long, gray German winters and would draw the heavy curtains and just live by lamp and candlelight. All of those lamps were covered with handmade silk shades, just like in Wustrow, and many of them had large, light pink and yellow silk roses around them.

Just when I thought that I could not take in anymore, just when I felt that there were too many things that were new and different and somewhat untouchable, my eyes came to rest on a brownish, bigger-than-life photograph hanging over my grandmother's desk in the living room. (I viewed that desk with some suspicion for many months. It had spindly, curvy legs, and I felt sure that the whole thing should collapse under the sheer weight of paper and pictures and vases with flowers, the ink well and scissors and pens and pencils, and a great big paperweight made of some green stony stuff. But the desk held firm, at least for the next fifteen years during which I saw it.)

I could not take my eyes off of the huge photograph. I tiptoed over to the picture and looked up to it rather reverently. It was of a young man in uniform. I could not see his full face, because the photograph was taken in profile. I did not know or understand that then, so I tiptoed to the side of the picture, trying to get him to look into my eyes, but that did not work. He just looked out the window, past me, past that beautiful room, past the world.

I whispered, "Who is it?" and my grandmother answered, "That is your *Onkel* Anton, your mother's oldest brother, my son, and he was killed in the war."

I did not know about World War I or what it had done to people. I sensed that it was something really sad because Oma had tears in her eyes. I ran over to her and into her open arms and let her hug me. I started to cry, too, and Oma said, "Tears are for us mothers and wives. Let's hope that you will grow up in a world where this can never happen again."

That was in 1931. In the following years we were spared nothing.

Later, I asked my mother to tell me about Onkel Anton and what it meant to have been killed in the war. My mother told me that Anton had been an air force pilot and had been in the *von Richthofen* squadron. The tail of his plane was painted red as a sign that he was with Richthofen. In the last days of the war his plane was sabotaged by Germans who cut the structure under the wings. He had no sooner taken off when he crashed to his death.

Mutti said, "We were very close, and I knew, without knowing how I knew, that he was dead the minute the plane crashed. I went to my parents and told them that Anton was dead. That occurred on November 9, 1918. The armistice was signed on November 11, but the telegram that told us that he had died on November 9 did not come until many days later."

I carried that thought with me for years, and whenever I was in the living room I tiptoed over to the huge picture, looked up at Onkel Anton, and thought of the plane with the red tail in which that handsome young man had crashed to his death.

That incredible living room was to become the waiting room for my mother's patients. During office hours a space was cleared, a screen from the bedroom was placed around the sofa and, with all the ancestors looking on, my mother would examine her patients.

In the beginning my mother did not have many patients, but during office hours, which were Mondays through Fridays from 10:00 a.m. to 11:00 a.m. and from 2:00 p.m. to 3:00 p.m., Oma and I sat in the little veranda behind her bedroom and continued the school studies we had started in Wustrow.

The chalk and slate were soon replaced with pencil and paper, numbers were introduced, and reading and doing number came along as a game. When I had had enough, my grandmother would pick up her knitting and prop up a book on her lap while I sat on the steps leading into the backyard. I was fascinated by the birds splashing around in the birdbath, and I watched the leaves and, later, the snowflakes fall.

Once in a while Oma would take me by the hand, and we'd walk to the corner to a tiny grocery store and drop off a shopping list with the owner, Paul Schulz. *Kaufmann* Schulz had a brother who was a fishmonger and another one who was a butcher. If there was sausage or meat or fish on our list, one of the grocer's three sons would run to their uncle's to pick up what was needed, and everything would be delivered to our house in the afternoon.

The only other store, which was not one of the Schulz enterprises, was the baker, who was just around the corner. Oma would take me there so that I could pick out one of their wonderful pastries, and she would take home a big loaf of dark rye bread, still warm from the oven.

It never occurred to me until years later that I was never out of my grandmother's sight for at least two years and that I never had a chance to play with other children, except for my cousins, whom Oma and I went to visit once a week; but that is another story.

An Unexpected Tenant

My mother did not have too much trouble building her practice, because she had grown up in the neighborhood and she collected money only when her patients could afford to pay. The early 1930s were hard in Germany and, as we know, all over the Western world. All of Oma's tenants came to pay their rent, and I became friends with all of them. Apart from the three apartments in Oma's house, there was one single room near the entrance that was rented to a single woman who said she was a seamstress. She was the only tenant I did not know.

When I was not studying with Oma I was outdoors on my scooter, riding up and down the bumpy sidewalk and, when I dared, all around the block. My grandmother did not like it when I rode around the block. She watched me all the time from the alcove in her living room for reasons I did not learn about until I was much older.

After a while, I noticed a man walking up and down the street, looking up at our windows. I knew him; his name was Altmüller, and he was a friend of my mother's.

Much, much later, I found out that Altmüller was a Communist— the old-fashioned kind, the kind that wanted nothing but the best for everybody without setting the world on fire and killing everybody who did not happen to agree. He had kept an eye on my mother since she was a teenager, especially since he knew that she was a member of the Social Democratic party and retained that membership even after Hitler disbanded the party and made membership illegal.

During the Nazi years Altmüller worked for us in the garden and sometimes slept in our basement, and the few Nazis in our neighborhood just left him alone. He probably worked with my mother in the Resistance and later was always in touch with her during the Russian occupation. To me he was just an old man who lived in the neighborhood, and I saw him practically every day. We said, "Good morning," to each other, and I rode away on my scooter, as he walked back and forth, looking up at our front windows.

One morning he stopped me and asked, "How is *Tante Doktor*?" All of the *Schweriners*, young and old, men and women alike, called her Tante Doktor, Auntie Doctor. Once, she even got a letter written by a child in the country, simply addressed to "Tante Doktor in Schwerin"!

I answered what all children answer, "Fine."

He asked, "Does she have many patients?"

"Oh, yes," I replied. "They are all waiting in Oma's living room, and that is why I have to play outside.

That evening I told my mother, "Altmüller is out there every day, and he is asking about your patients."

"We'll see about that," said my mother, and the next day she confronted Altmüller, and from what I can gather, the following conversation ensued:

"Altmüller, why are you watching this house and asking my daughter about my patients?"

"Tante Doktor, I thought you were a children's kind of a doctor, and I worry about all the men going in and out of your house."

"What men? I see mostly children and often their mothers, too, because I can't treat a child without knowing how crazy the mother is."

"Tante Doktor, there is a man going into your house and one coming out, just about every half hour."

You guessed it!

Our little seamstress from the room near the entrance was engaging in the world's oldest profession, right next door to my grandmother's bedroom.

I overheard the conversation between my mother and grandmother but did not understand too much of it.

I realized that my mother was shocked, while my grandmother was laughing until the tears were running down her cheeks.

Needless to say, the little seamstress had to go, and her room became my mother's examining room and office because it was so conveniently located. Her camp bed came down from the loft and became the examining couch, which is also where my mother slept during the night.

Secrets

For about two years I slept in my grandmother's bedroom behind a flowered screen on the softest, coziest sofa imaginable. My mother was out almost every evening, "making house calls," I was told.

But late every night, she came to my bed behind the screen to hug me and say, "Good night," then she would sit by my grandmother's bed and tell her about her day and what was happening in the outside world.

They never realized that I was listening to every word during all those nights while I slept in my grandmother's room. The eavesdropping stopped only when my mother could afford to rent the rest of the house from her mother, and I got my own room.

I got my early anti-Nazi education listening to those two talk to each other from 1931 to 1933. I heard that people were beaten up by hoodlums, members of the *Sturmabteilung*, also known as the SA—Hitler's Storm Troopers.

I remember one incident in particular when my mother had been hiding outside a meeting of the *Stahlhelm Bund* (Steel Helmet League), a right-wing organization composed of veterans of the

First World War. These veterans objected to the rise of the Nazis.

There were other organizations who also objected to the Nazi doctrine, such as the hiking club *Wandervögel* and other sport clubs, the National Socialist Party, and the Communist Party. They all got together at secret meeting places to discuss what to do about the Nazis.

To my mother, it was clear that Hitler's Storm Troopers infiltrated these meetings and then beat people up severely. She would wait outside, and when it was all over she would go in and tend to the wounded.

The significance of all of this did not become clear to me until about fifty years later when I had a conversation with my lifelong best friend, Gerda Keller. Gerda's father, an officer in the First World War, had been a member of the Stahlhelm Bund. He came home one night, very badly beaten about the head, saying that a woman doctor had suddenly appeared out of nowhere and treated everybody's wounds.

Fourteen years after the Great War, Hans Keller was a civilian. Many years later, in 1945, he was the major who surrendered our town, without a fight, to the Americans. Gerda was able to supply me with all the details of the surrender—but we are not there yet.

It seems funny now that I never asked about the whispered conversations and always carried those fears and worries quietly in my heart. I think that I was very curious and wanted to know what was going on in the big outside world, and I was afraid that those conversations would stop if they knew that I was listening.

I was ready to start school in April of 1933, when I would have been six and a half years old, but on January 31—one day after Hitler came to power—my mother announced, "You are not going to start school this spring."

When I asked in astonishment why I could not start school, she answered, "Because you are too small."

I did not ask any further questions because I sensed, even then, that there were bad things happening, and I also knew that I would find out eventually by listening to those nightly conversations.

Actually, I was not much taller when I finally started school a year later.

I was, and remained, nearly the smallest in class, always at the far end of the lineup of students. The true reason for my delayed school entry became clear soon enough. I heard that my father was leaving the country for political reasons and that it would be best if I were kept in the house for the next few months until things simmered down.

My grandmother continued my home schooling, and by the time I started school at age seven and a half, I could read and write and do simple arithmetic. I could knit and crochet and had listened to Oma reading the classic books. She loved Goethe's *Faust* and played piano pieces by Mendelssohn, Offenbach, and other Jewish composers because she knew that I would not get to hear those once I was in public school.

As my understanding of what I overheard grew, I knew that the Nazis had disbanded all political parties, the trade unions, and all clubs and organizations that had any kind of political agenda. The only party that remained was the far right wing National Socialist Party, whose name had been changed to the *Nationalsozialistische Deutsche Arbeiterpartei*—the National Socialist Workers Party of Germany, also known as the Nazi Party, or NSDAP—and for some this became sort of a trade union.

I cannot go into all the reasons why people joined; I have always felt that it was either for personal gain or out of fear. The party claimed to be antimodern, anticapitalist, anticommunist, and antisemitic. In short, it claimed to be against everything that could be blamed for the misery in Germany and the Western world in general.

My mother remained a member of the Social Democratic Party until her death in 1981. During the twelve years of the Nazi reign, the party members went underground, and in deepest secrecy they formed a resistance movement. The purpose was to help all those who were persecuted by the Nazis. That included not only Jews, but also Gypsies, homosexuals, people with physical or mental disorders and, of course, all of those who openly dared to oppose the system. My mother took a leading, coordinating position within that resistance group in Schwerin.

It was around this time, in the spring of 1933, that I asked my grandmother about what I had heard at night, and she answered and explained every question. She also said to my mother something like, "There is no point in us whispering while she is behind the curtain. She hears us anyway, and since she has to live with it, she might as well get it right."

After that, at age six and a half, I was included in all the grown-up conversations, and I learned, very early, what I could repeat and what must be kept a secret. You might think that I was too young for all this, but since I was bright and extremely curious, this was done for my own safety, and I held up pretty well under it.

Sometime in 1935, when I was nine years old, my grand-mother sat me down and explained to me about the newly enacted Nuremberg Laws. These laws stated that anyone who had a Jewish grandparent was considered to have enough Jewish blood to be unwelcome in the new Germany. She told me that my father had a Jewish grandmother, and that was why he left Germany in the spring of 1933.

Oma kept impressing upon me that I was just one-sixteenth Jewish, that I had only around 12 percent Jewish blood, and that I had to remember this fact when people started to tease me, bump into me, and call me a *Judenmädchen* (Jew girl).

My great-grandmother was Jewish!

Bless Oma! I believed her for fifty years. I did hear in later years that, except for my grandmother and me, anybody who knew us at all, including our own family, believed that my father was a Jew. My grandmother gave me tremendous confidence and self-assurance; it was that and my mother's great connections in the community that kept me safe during the Holocaust.

Many years later, when it was all over, I was told repeatedly by family and friends that they had stuck with me even though they had "known" that my father was a Jew.

When DNA testing became widely available in 2014, I had myself tested, and I was found to have 12 percent Ashkenazi genes, which means that, indeed, I have a Jewish great-grandparent. My grandmother had been right all along!

My mother never spoke to me about my father. It was as if he never existed, and over the years my memory of him as a father faded—and with such a strong mother who trusted me completely and such a loving and caring grandmother, I never missed him.

I was told early in my life whom I had to fear. The list was long for such a little person.

First of all, there were the Nazi Party members. There were so many of them, and I was told to remember their names. Actually, many people belonged to the Nazi Party for political gain and safety and did not do us any harm. They did not realize that they supported a criminal and intolerable system. It was just that you could not trust them and had to watch every word you said.

And then there was the SA, which functioned as the original paramilitary wing of the Nazi Party. To me, they were men in ugly brown, baby-poop-colored uniforms with funny hats, and they were to be avoided. They beat people with their sticks and arrested people for no reason. You did not talk to them, and you crossed the street when you saw one. Fortunately for me, there were very few SA, and they lived in another part of town.

The last group to be really feared was the SS, the *Schutzstaffel*, Hitler's Elite. They were the "Security Police." They wore smashing black uniforms with a skull emblem on their shoulders and on their caps. The skull was frightening enough, but it was those super-shiny black boots with, I think, metal on the heels, which scared me the most. I can still hear their rhythmic marching sound, and I was not allowed to show how scared I was, because they were supposed to be our protectors.

Those SS men were ruthless, threatening, and when one of them entered a house he "filled the door," and everybody's heart started to tremble with fear.

I learned much later, when I was about twelve, that their leader was Heinrich Himmler, who ruled over the shadowy world of death and extermination camps. His SS created the infrastructure that would make the Holocaust possible.

Fortunately for me and the rest of us, the SS did not enter my life too much, and there were not many of them in Schwerin at that time. There was nothing for them to do except to assemble once in a while and yell, "*Heil* Hitler!" At least, that is how my mother explained it to calm me.

I saw those SS creatures only from afar, I am glad to say, and really not until the very end of the war, when the beasts had to flee for their lives, take off their uniforms, and try to hide in our fairly safe and undestroyed city.

But I recall meeting one of those men when I was about seven.

He was the brother of our housemaid, and while he was on leave in Schwerin, he asked to take Wilma and me to a café. My grandmother, not knowing that Wilma's brother was in the SS and certainly not expecting him to call in full uniform, gave permission for the visit to the café.

When the doorbell rang I raced down the stairs, two flights of them, and when I opened the door, there stood this huge creature dressed all in black with those shiny black boots, a wide red swastika band around his left arm, and a skull on his cap. To me this sight was very frightening, and I thought my heart would stop as I was holding onto the front door.

He took off his cap, tucked it under his arm, and said, "I am Gus, Wilma's brother, and I have come to take you to a *Konditorei*."

He turned out to be very nice, and after filling me up with meringue and whipped cream, my favorite to this day, and after having a nice chat with his sister, he took us home. Wilma married the next year, and I never saw Gus again.

As far as I can recall, that was the last time I had my fill of whipped cream, because in 1936 the regime decided that rearmament and war were inevitable, and a system of rationing dairy products began. Please don't ask me why dairy products, because I don't know. All I know is that the German people were supposed to have voted that they wanted *Kanonen für Butter*— Guns Instead of Butter.

Cousins

Oma had another daughter, Elsbeth Anna, known to me as Tante Eische, who had married one of my mother's fellow medical students. She and her husband, Hermann Strauss, lived in Schwerin with their two children, Tom and Dorli, and it was shortly after we arrived in Schwerin that Oma took me by the hand and we walked to their house. It was about a twenty-minute walk through the town and up the Moltke *Strasse* into the Lübecker Strasse.

The house was a single house, very unusual for a German town, and was right next to a railroad track—not considered one of the best locations these days, but oh, how I enjoyed staying overnight when the trains came thundering by and made the whole building shake.

The Strauss family lived upstairs. The lower floor was Hermann's medical practice, which he had inherited from his father, who had been one of the leading physicians and a *Sanitätsrat* in town. That title impressed me no end. Hermann's father, who died several years ago, was always referred to as *Der Herr Sanitätsrat*. My mother explained to me, a few years later, that the title of Sanitätsrat was bestowed by the Grand

Duke or some other royal potentate and was totally meaningless after Germany became a republic at the end of the First World War. It impressed only the wife, her bridge club, the butcher, the baker, and the gardener.

Tante Eische stood at the top of the stairs, called Tom and Dorli, and said, "Löttken is here."

I'll never forget that moment for as long as I live. I loved being called Löttken, a Northern German diminutive of Charlotte, instead of that harsh *Lotte*, or worse yet, *Lotti*. (There are more cows named Lotti than I care to remember.)

The three of us—Tom, Dorli, and I—took to each other as ducks to water. Tom was about one year older than I, and Dorli was six months younger. Tante Eische and my cousins accepted me as a member of the family, as their little sister (I continued to be shorter than everyone else).

Dorli and I became the best of friends—a friendship that would last a lifetime, spanning continents and incredible political differences, until she died in my arms sixty years later, riddled with cancer.

The children had two rooms. The bedroom was a narrow one with an oval window, and the room was always referred to as the *Ochsenauge*, the ox eye. There were two beds placed end to end, a chest of drawers, and a sink. I slept in Tom's bed when I visited, which was often; Dorli slept in the other one. I have no idea where Tom slept, and I am afraid Dorli and I did not much care. The arrangement was much easier after Tom got his own room in the loft about a year later.

The ox eye was on the side of the house nearest the railroad track, and when I close my eyes, I can still feel the rhythmic rocking of the trains thundering by. That is where I had my first dreams of just getting on a train and going and going all around the world.

The other room was the playroom. The Strauss family was well-to-do, and the children had a large number of toys and a *Kindermädchen*, a nanny, who kept things tidy and supplied us with whatever we thought we needed, such as watercolors, scissors and paper, beads and string, and stacks of coloring books.

Dorli was a quiet little girl who accepted the fact that I did not care to play with dolls or soldiers and that I chattered constantly.

We ate with the household staff in the large and sunny central hall under a huge skylight. In the middle of the hall stood an octagonal table with a wooden tabletop, which was scrubbed white.

I was so impressed.

Only once in a while, such as on holidays, birthdays, or when there was a special visitor, the three of us were allowed to eat in the dining room with the grown-ups. Come to think of it, my grandmother was always there when I was there, but my mother was a rare and special visitor.

The reason for that did not become clear to me until years later.

We must have been allowed to eat at the *Männertisch* (the men's table) many times, but actually I remember only one of these occasions clearly, and it must have happened when we were six or seven years old.

Dorli and I always sat next to each other, which was probably not the best plan, because I was forever teasing—kicking Dorli under the table, rolling my eyes and squinting, or balancing an incredible amount of food on a tiny piece of bread and then making a great to-do about getting it into my mouth. Dorli always tried to keep a straight face because she was much more afraid of her father than I was.

Once she tried to take a swallow of her cocoa, and in her effort to swallow it while also trying to suppress her laughter, the cocoa came out of her nose in two brown streams. For a minute that stopped me, and I was just getting ready to clap my hands when Onkel Hermann's fist came down on the table so hard that it made the glasses dance.

He just said one word, *"Raus,"* (Out!) and pointed to the door.

As I was leaving, I saw that Oma had covered her mouth with her serviette and was shaking with laughter. A pale Tante Eische came out into the hall and told us to sit on the staircase leading to the attic. We sat there for only a minute or two, when the door opened again and Tom swaggered out with his bony knees in his lederhosen. He said that it was no fun being in there without us.

In 1934 Tante Eische had a new baby, a little boy called Helmut. The baby was born at home, and when I visited the next day, in his tiny crib were three colorful bags, each with a name tag: Tom, Dorli, and Löttken. I can't remember what was in the bags, probably sweets and little gifts, but the important thing for me was that I was always included, that I was a member of that family, and that I had brothers and sisters.

Helmut was baptized in the *Paulskirche* (St. Paul's Church), which was right behind the house along a narrow path, called the *Katzensteig* (cat's path), beside the railroad track. You had to walk along the path and up a few steps to get to the church. We made quite a procession.

There were four churches in Schwerin, and eventually they all became Nazi churches, as my mother called them—they held services, collected their tax (in Germany, the state and the church are not separated), and subscribed to the Nazi doctrine. This meant that Jesus Christ, the Jew, was never mentioned, but you heard the name of Adolf Hitler a lot. The churches got their tax money in return for a promise to cooperate fully with the Nazi system, which they did, to my mother's disgust.

In 1934 and '35 the churches had not changed yet, and it is possible that my mother even attended Helmut's baptism.

In 1936 another baby was born.

This time it was a little girl, Gudrun, and again there was that wonderful little bag with goodies for all of us. Only, I no longer believed that the baby had actually brought those bags. I knew where babies came from and even had a vague idea how they got there. By then I was ten and could read, and my mother had a lot of books in her medical practice and never hesitated to answer my questions.

I don't remember how and where Gudrun was baptized, but since it was 1936, it might very well have been in St. Paul's Church.

Then, in November 1938, came Ute—that lovely little girl, my most talented ballet student, the elegant hostess whom I visited in New York and Singapore, my best travel companion to Bali and Java, to New Delhi and Jaipur. The little girl who grew tall and slim, married a fabulous man, and put her arm around me protectively when some of the local men in those faraway places became too pushy.

There is just one thing that Ute and I cannot discuss to this day: her father, my Onkel Hermann, was a convinced and dedicated Nazi. He spent endless hours in medical service to the Hitler Youth and, unlike my mother, was part of the socialized medicine team and had a very large practice, tending to his patients with loving care.

And yet, he attended Wagner opera performances in full Nazi uniform; traveled for rallies to Nürnberg and München; and made regular visits to the *Sachsenberg*, the local insane asylum where one of the Nazi euthanasia programs was conducted. I did not then and I do not now understand these two sides of my onkel.

Uta was baptized in December 1938 or January 1939. Oma and I were invited, and my mother was, as usual, conspicuous by her absence. Onkel Hermann stood in full uniform under Hitler's picture in the living room, holding Ute in his arms. He touched his hand to her forehead and said, *"Ich taufe Dich Ute, die*

Sippentochter " (I baptize you Ute, the Daughter of the Clan). I was twelve years old at the time; we had just come through *Kristallnacht*, and I felt that there was something bizarre about this baptism.

My mother never said a word when I told her what happened, just nodded her head, and I am glad. The Strauss family was my family, and I loved them.

Many years later, I understood how very hard all of this must have been on everyone.

After my father left Germany because everyone believed that he was a Jew, Onkel Hermann had two choices: either get rid of me—which would have been an easy thing because all he had to do was denounce me as a half-Jew—or go along with my grand-mother and declare to everybody that my father had a Jewish grandmother, which according to the Nuremberg Laws would have made him one-quarter Jew and therefore persona non grata in Hitler's Germany, but I was okay.

To make sure that he could not be accused of shielding a "black sheep," using his Nazi connections, he had all the papers con-nected to my father's family, the Marienfelds of Berlin, de-stroyed. When I wanted to find out about my father's family, which had lived in Berlin for generations, I could find no refer-ence to the Marienfelds.

Hermann did refer to me as the black sheep on occasion, which got back to me. My mother was also well aware of this, but nobody in the Strauss family ever let me feel that I did not really belong, so I led this happy double life. But I was always aware that I was different.

Gypsies and Carnivals

After my father left the country in the spring of 1933, I was finally allowed to go about freely. Many years later, my mother told me that she had been afraid that my father would kidnap me and take me with him, out of Germany and away from the Nazis, whom he hated and feared.

She was also afraid that harm would come to me because he had a Jewish grandmother. That fear never left her, and as soon as I was able to understand, she and Oma shared that fear with me. This hung like a cloud over my head all through my teenage years and did not leave until the Nazis were finally defeated.

Even so, I felt like a little bird whose cage door had been opened, and I roamed the neighborhood. There was a lake right at the bottom of our street, and I would sit on the shore and watch the ducks, wondering who lived in the houses on the other side. Behind our block was a large, open field where, during week-ends, they had football matches. Two or three times a year the carnival came to town, and it was set up so close to our house that we could hear the music coming in through the always-open windows.

Curious as I was, I was a constant visitor to the carnival, and by the time they had the roundabouts, the swings, and the tents all set up, the carnival people knew me. And once the fair got going, there was always someone there to lift me up onto one of those beautiful wooden horses on the carousel, and I went round and round for as long as I wanted.

I got in to see the fat lady, and I visited her so often that she started to smile at me, but she never said a word. Then there was the man who swallowed fire; to this day, I have never been able to figure out just how he did it.

It never occurred to me that other people had to pay money to do and see these things. I just went around, looked in every tent, inspected the horses, sat with the children, and was always greeted with a smile and often a handshake. What I did not know and, like many other things, found out years later, was that my mother always went to the carnival manager as soon as the carnival came to town and offered her medical services. She would tell them where her office was, only a block away, and if necessary, she would go into their caravans and visit the sick.

In retrospect, I can imagine the reaction of the patients who waited in my grandmother's elegant living room to see my mother. When a man or woman from the carnival arrived with a child or two, they quietly took a seat and waited their turn. You could tell carnival people because they dressed differently. Even so, there was not ever a single complaint, and I can only explain that by saying that my mother knew her patients and, what is even more important, the patients knew and respected my mother.

This was important because under the Nazi system, what my mother was doing was illegal and therefore dangerous. The Nazis wanted people to register, have a permanent address, and become part of the tax and health insurance system. My mother was undermining that system, and the local medical association took a dim view of her work.

One evening—it must have been in the fall of 1933 because it got dark quite early—just as I was putting my scooter away, I noticed a reddish glow in the sky behind one of the houses at the end of the street. I remember this as clearly as if it happened yesterday. I went around that house, started to tiptoe, then stopped in awe.

There, around a huge fire, sat a number of grown-ups and children, dressed in strange-looking clothing. They were Gypsies, but I did not know that. I looked from face to face. The fire was reflected in their liquid eyes, and they were all looking at me. Except for the crackling of the fire, there was total silence.

It must have been quite a sight: this tiny person, in her little brown boots and camel hair coat, looking at this wonder, with eyes every bit as large and brown as theirs.

After a little while, one of the women got up, put her arm around me, and asked, "Do you want to sit with us?" I just nodded because I was too overcome to speak.

The children moved around a little and made a space for me in the circle, and there we sat, in total silence. Maybe it was not for as long as I remember it to be, but finally a man with long, black, shiny hair in braids, got up, picked up a forked stick, and poked it in the fire. He brought up a black, round thing and put it on the ground next to one of the women, and she took a wooden fork and opened it up. I could see steam escape. It was the first baked potato I had ever seen in my life.

The man brought out more and more of those black potatoes, and pretty soon everybody had one. At that point he made wordless eye contact with me, and I nodded excitedly and got a baked potato just like everyone else. The wooden fork was passed around, everyone split their potato, and when the boy next to me got the fork, he looked at me, started to grin, and split my potato for me.

Even the rising steam had a wonderful smell. When the potato had cooled off, I, who had been taught to eat with my grand-mother's heavy table silver, followed everyone's example and nibbled and sucked the delicious stuff right out of the blackened skin. It was the best baked potato I ever ate in all my life!

There still was not a word, but suddenly I saw everyone looking in one direction, and there was my mother, standing in the fire's glow. She was waving her hand in greeting, and everyone raised their hand in greeting too. She quietly walked over, took me by the hand, waved again, and we walked home in silence.

It was not until years later that I wondered how other parents would have reacted under the same circumstances.

My mother was different; her contact with other human beings was different. She taught me to recognize and appreciate the dignity in everyone. Today I understand that her view was like the Buddhist *namaste*, which means, "My soul bows to your soul," and she taught me to live by that principle. She also taught me to be careful and to learn to *smell*—I am sure she meant *recognize*, but she did say smell—a Nazi, however disguised.

That was the last time the Gypsies came to town, because after 1933 the Nazis started to round them up. Gypsies had never been popular with the German government, which did not approve of their nomadic lifestyle. Germans did not like nomads. (Incidentally, nobody called them *Roma* then). Just as with the carnival and circus people, the government wanted everybody to be registered and fully integrated into the tax, school, and health systems. Even to this day, you have to be registered in the town in which you live, and you have to give notification if you move away. Imagine the chaos ten and twenty years later, when thousands of persecuted people secretly and illegally fled Eastern Germany.

The Nazis detested Gypsies as much as Jews. They saw the Gypsies as a foreign, inferior race, people inappropriate to mix with the Aryan Germans. It was easy for the Nazis to determine who was a Jew, because the Jews were all duly registered in the books of the synagogues, while the approximately thirty thousand Gypsies in Germany were almost exclusively Roman Catholic, and the Catholic Church did not keep a record of races. So the Nazis rounded them all up, just for their appearance and for living like nomads, put them in concentration camps, and eventually murdered them, along with six million Jews.

My fascination with Gypsies has stayed with me all my life, and when I hear a Hungarian Rhapsody, I see that big fire and those glistening eyes.

My mother continued to do her illegal medical work, and she continued, openly, to refuse to join the Nazi Party. Because of that, she was not permitted to participate in the excellent German health insurance program, and all her patients were either private patients or treated pro bono.

You did not have to hide Jews in your basement to be a true Resistance worker, and to this day I am so very proud of my mother.

The New House

By 1936, my mother's medical practice had grown sufficiently so that she was able to buy a new house. Well, the house was built in 1898, but it was much larger than my grandmother's house, closer to a tram stop and a pharmacy, and still in the "right part of town," which was important for her practice to continue growing.

The house had a basement, two stories, and a loft. The first story was home to the medical offices, the second story contained the living quarters plus the kitchen, and the loft had two finished rooms—my bedroom and the staff bedroom. The first two floors had four large rooms, each with a twelve-foot ceiling. The large windows in the front had a view of Bismarck Square, while the rooms in the back had balconies and looked out into the backyard, which was so large and had so many chestnut and fruit trees that you could not see any of the neighboring houses.

My mother's offices were on the first floor. The living room, dining room, and my mother's bedroom were on the second floor. One large room on that floor was divided into my mother's bathroom and the kitchen. Those two facilities had been in the basement before, I am sure.

There was a toilet down in the dark basement that was used by the patients, and a gloomy thing it was. Our upstairs toilet, which I am sure my mother had installed, was halfway up the stairs between the first and second floors.

More about that little toilet later, because it became so important in our lives for the next nine long years, until the end of the war, after the Nazis were finally gone.

My bedroom was way up in the loft, big and bright, and the view from my windows was directly into a huge chestnut tree. I could follow the seasons by observing first the sticky buds, then the beautiful, candle-like blossoms, and by seeing the leaves change color from spring's most tender green to summer's dark green. The tree shaded my room for all the summer months and made me feel safe and protected. In fall, the leaves turned to brown, and in winter the branches stood bare and still, making me wish for spring. That tree became part of my often lonely and, yes, dangerous life.

I had a modern couch, which made into a bed, and a writing bureau and a piano, which I played as little as possible. Seven years of piano lessons were totally wasted on me except for some knowledge of harmony and theory. But I loved my gramophone! No, I did not play the *Schlager*, the hit tunes of the day. I had a great selection of arias and overtures from operas and operettas, and my favorite of all, Viennese waltzes.

My bedroom was my sanctuary and the hangout for me and my girlfriends. Since the room had an extra bed, there was always someone who was only too glad to stay over. After all, no one else had a gramophone!

Next door was the maids' room, and we always had a house-keeper and one or two household helpers. I have no idea how they felt about that gramophone going on at all hours, but that is how it was in those days. I was the doctor's daughter, the little princess. Actually, that status had a lot of drawbacks because I was never let into the kitchen, did not learn how to cook, and did not have a clue about how to do dishes or clean a kitchen sink.

In those days it was difficult to get an actual telephone, and my mother, as a physician, had to apply for a special permit. Since the house was not wired for a telephone and since we needed a phone in every room, we had phone jacks installed wherever necessary. We had one permanent telephone unit in my mother's office, and we carried the second unit from room to room as needed.

Not long after we moved into our new home, one of my mother's patients, a young man who worked for the telephone company, came to her office, ostensibly for a sore throat. When she said to him, "I can't see anything wrong," he put his finger to his lips and whispered, "Can we go into the garden?" My mother, by now used to strange things, nodded, and they both went out the back door and disappeared between the bushes.

"Every one of those phone jacks we installed in your house has a bug in it. Your phone has been monitored for a long time, but now they can hear what you say in every room, whether you are on the phone or not. Don't let them find out that you know this, or it will be my neck."

We lived with that for almost ten years and, young as I was, I knew what could be discussed and what had to be kept quiet. My mother and I kept our conversation as normal as possible. In fact, with the exception of Minna, our faithful housekeeper, the household staff never found out about this strange condition in our house.

I mentioned earlier that my mother had had a toilet installed halfway up the stairs between the first and second floors. That tiny space, with a tiny window, was the only safe spot in our house. My mother and I would squeeze into that little room, and I would have to literally flatten myself against the wall while my mother sat, and that way we could safely talk about what we could not afford to let the rest of the world know.

As I got older and participated more in my mother's underground and dangerously illegal activities, we spent more and more time in that little space. I do not have the vaguest idea what our staff thought of mother and daughter going so frequently to the lavatory together. Actually, we had our best mother-daughter talks in that tiny toilet.

I visited our house forty years later, after the Berlin Wall had fallen and it was possible to visit East Germany. My grandson Chris was with me, and I had contacted the new owners and asked them if we might visit and take pictures of the places I had talked so much about. Their e-mailed reply came immediately, and we were cordially invited. Our little safe space was now a broom closet in the totally remodeled house. One of the daughters was concerned that I might be upset because the door had recently been painted green.

No one can possibly imagine what memories that visit to our house brought back. I was so grateful to have Chris, that eager photographer, by my side.

The Olympic Games in Berlin

In the spring of 1936, just as I had begun grade three and we were settled in our new house, the talk about the Olympic Games, which were to be held in Berlin for the first two weeks in August, started both in school and on the radio. I am sure that the newspaper was also full of news and anticipation, but since the politically neutral *Mecklenburger Zeitung* had had to close its door and only the Nazi paper, *Der Völkische Beobachter*, was available, no newspaper ever crossed our doorstep.

Nazi Germany wanted to use the 1936 Olympic Games as propaganda for the new, strong and united Germany, and for two weeks in August, Adolf Hitler's dictatorship masked its racist and militaristic character.

The compulsory signs on stores that said *Keine Juden* (no Jews) were taken down; and six hundred Gypsies were rounded up and their wagons with their inhabitants taken to an open field near a cemetery and a sewage dump in a place called Marzahn, east of Berlin.

As usual, my Onkel Hermann and his family rented a small house at the Baltic Sea near Warnemünde for the duration of the school holidays. This happened to be during the time of the Olympic Games. I was invited to come along and was very excited about that.

My uncle came to stay with us for long weekends, but my mother never did. In my memory I have a tendency to put a political slant on everything, because that is just how it was in our house. But the reason my mother never came was probably because she and my uncle could not both be out of town at the same time. There would be no one left in Schwerin to tend to their patients.

Strangely enough, although I was ten years old, I don't remember anything about playing on the beach or being in the water, but I do remember every bit of listening to the Olympics on the radio while sitting on the patio of the little rented cottage with my cousins, Tom and Dorli, eating ice cream and drinking lemonade.

What I did not know then, but what my mother got across to me after my return, was that Hitler saw the link with the ancient Greek games as the perfect way to illustrate his belief that classical Greece was an Aryan forerunner of the modern Third Reich.

It is not commonly known that bringing the Olympic torch by relay from Greece to the Olympic city was pioneered by the Nazis and was carefully supervised by Joseph Goebbels, the minister of propaganda. The run started on July 20, 1936, in Olympia, Greece; passed through Bulgaria, Yugoslavia, Hungary, Austria, and Czechoslovakia; and arrived punctually on August 1.

Two urns were lit by a young runner named Siegfried Eifrig.

I shall never forget that name. *Siegfried* is so very Germanic, and *eifrig* means eager. With all that was going on, I wonder whether that blond and Aryan-looking young man was not also chosen for his name, or whether the name was changed for the occasion.

For us children, having to listen to those broadcasts of the flame being carried from country to country was kind of boring, but it was a good lesson in geography. We had a big map and took turns circling, with a red pencil, every town the flame passed through.

We could follow the route of the flame at least one more time after the release of the films of the Olympic Games by Hitler's greatly admired photographer, Leni Riefenstahl. These films were required viewing at least once in all schools, and we also had to write essays about the races and know the names of the German winners.

 Little did anyone know then that all the countries through which the torch had passed would fall under Nazi domination during the Second World War, which would begin less than three years later.

Naturally, it was a great deal of fun listening to the broadcasts of the races and the excited, almost breathless commentators, but it seems to me in retrospect that we heard only about those competitions in which the Germans were winning, because after the second or third day, we youngsters took it for granted that the Germans would win.

There was just one exception.

Even before the actual games started, we had heard about the great American athlete, Jesse Owens. He was greatly admired by those Germans who had not been influenced by the Nazi propaganda and did not care about the color of any person's skin. He achieved international fame with the four gold medals he won, and he was the most successful athlete at the games.

He was credited with single-handedly crushing Hitler's myth of Aryan supremacy.

Not too much was said about that at the time, especially not in my uncle's presence, but my mother explained it all to me in our secret little space.

Hitler did not attend any medal ceremonies after Jesse Owens' spectacular performance, but right after the games, Albert Speer—famous for being Hitler's architect and later the Minister of Armaments and War Production—wrote, "Hitler was highly annoyed by the series of triumphs by the colored American runner, Jesse Owens. However, he just shrugged his shoulders and said that people whose antecedents came from the jungle were primitive, their physiques were stronger than those of civilized whites and hence, they should be excluded from future games."

Only a few days after the games, when all the visitors had left, the Nazis restarted their hate, extermination, and expansionist policies with a vengeance. The signs saying Keine Juden returned to the store windows; butter was rationed; more Gypsies, homosexuals, and any opponents to the Nazi policies were rounded up and put into camps; and foreign travel was severely restricted.

The handwriting was on the wall, for those who could see it.

Ballet

After Hitler's successful Olympics, he and his cohorts were basking in the sun of the huge, political success the Nazis had achieved. Simultaneously, they had been able to hide the fear and the impending suffering of the people in Germany from the rest of the world.

My mother could see what was coming; she was sure that the Nazis were there to stay and that they would do incredible damage to all of Europe.

She also knew that unless she was able to prevent it, I would be automatically enrolled into the *Jungmädchen* (Nazi Young Girls) when I turned ten and entered the fourth grade, and she knew that she had to protect me and find a way to keep me from having to participate in any Hitler Youth activities.

She had already managed to put off that date for me by one year, by changing my birth year, and I had not started school until I was seven and a half. She was the school physician and did not have to provide documentation for enrolling her daughter in school.

My mother's solution to keep me out of the grasp of the Nazis was brilliant, and she turned the next six years, in spite of what was happening all around, into the happiest years of my young life.

It was in late September of 1936 that my mother walked with me into the office of Madam Pinkepank (yes, that was her name), the ballet mistress at the *Schweriner Staats Theater,* the State Theater of Schwerin, and enrolled me into the *Kinder Ballet,* the Children's Ballet.

Madam Pinkepank and my mother looked into each other's eyes and shook hands, I curtsied, and I was in. I was accepted without having to dance, do any gymnastics, or read any lines.

It pays to have connections.

After that, I attended ballet classes twice a week after school, and in retrospect I am so glad that they did not change the name of the ballet steps from French into German. Normally the Nazis did not permit any foreign words in their language. The international language of ballet is French, and that is how I learned my ballet steps.

The first half of the lesson consisted of bar exercises, and they actually had to lower one short bar just for me. I held on to that bar for six years, even after I had grown tall enough to reach the regular ones when I was fourteen.

The ballet lessons were free, and we children were used in crowd scenes; sang when the children's chorus was required; and also took children's parts, either acting, dancing, or singing.

I was a choirboy in *Cavalleria Rusticana,* a street urchin in *Carmen,* a *Nibelung* in *Das Rheingold,* and the mustard seed in *Midsummer Night's Dream* and danced my way through a long list of operas and operettas.

Best of all, nobody seemed to mind that I stood in the wings and watched every performance from beginning to end. On the day of a performance, I always arrived early, applied my makeup quickly, and ran down the many stairs to the stage just as the performance started. As soon as I finished my part, I dashed upstairs, quickly removed my makeup, put on my street clothes, and was back in the wings again until the end of the performance.

Nobody else did that, and in those six years I remember only twice being brought by a stagehand to the stage director, who said, *"Das ist doch die kleine Hugues"* (This is the little Hugues.), which implied that I was the daughter of Dr. Hugues, and that was my passport to everything.

My mother was the house physician, who was called in for emergencies and treated any of the theater staff free of charge. On occasion, she was also seen sitting in the loge with the theater manager and his wife. None of the other ballet girls had those kind of connections, and the ballet, the theater, and all of that wonderful music helped me through those difficult and dangerous years ahead.

Anschluss of Austria

After the Olympic Games in 1936, travel outside of Germany became practically impossible. You needed a visa to go anywhere, and your reasons for going were closely examined. Every trip abroad went on your record, and if any Nazi could possibly interpret your journey as having a political connection, you could be arrested and questioned. Although things were really mellow in Schwerin in comparison to other parts of Germany, my mother never took the chance to apply for a foreign travel visa.

On March 12, 1938, Austria was annexed by Nazi Germany. They called it the *Anschluss,* and it had disastrous consequences for Austrian Jews. Nazi anti-Semitism was much more vicious in Austria, especially in Vienna where 10 percent of the population was either Jewish or married to a Jew. To this day, it is hard for me to understand why the Austrians hated the Jews to that extent, especially when they had contributed so much to Austrian culture.

There was a strong resistance group in Austria, and I suppose that the only contact with them that my mother was able to make was by whispered word of mouth and by courier.

Little did I know that four years later, I would become such a courier myself.

About ten days after the Anschluss, my mother and I boarded a train to Munich, and from there to Innsbruck, Austria. The Nazis wanted to demonstrate to the Germans how delighted the Austrians were to be incorporated into the German Reich; therefore, no visa was needed. In fact, travel to Austria was now encouraged, and the Nazis never suspected why this now prosperous woman doctor was taking so many vacations.

I was excited and enjoyed my train trip tremendously, but I soon sensed that this was much more than just a vacation or an opportunity for me to see the world. My mother had too many quiet conversations with people she appeared to know, and I felt that there was a connection that I did not yet understand.

After that first trip, we traveled to Austria regularly in the spring and fall until 1942. By that time, when so many doctors were needed at the front, my mother's services were needed at home. Many of the younger male doctors had been drafted, and as one of the few remaining physicians—and the one with by far the largest practice—it would have looked strange if she had taken too many vacations.

In 1942 I was sixteen and very mature for my age. I knew to a large extent what was going on and was proud to take over as a courier. Our destination in Austria was always Seefeld in Tirol, a well-known ski resort just north of Innsbruck. We stayed at the same beautiful old hotel, the *Klosterbräu.*

Two or three hundred years earlier, the hotel had been a monastery with a brewery. There had been substantial renovations on the floors where the restaurants and guest rooms were, but since I was free to roam and explore the long, dark hallways and the cellars, to me it was much more like a mysterious old monastery than a hotel. At that time, I did not know that that old hotel, with all its dark and secret passages, was also one of the headquarters of the Austrian Resistance.

Years later, after the war and after Austria had become an independent country again, I returned, and the Klosterbräu was an elegant, expensive, remodeled hotel—and all of the romance was gone.

Of course, that very first trip to Austria is the one that comes to mind almost eighty years later when I think of Austria.

Since we had moved from East Prussia to Mecklenburg seven years previously, we really had not traveled at all except for our summers at the Baltic coast and some trips into the Harz Mountains.

On our first journey to Seefeld, as we approached the Austrian Alps by train from Munich I saw what I thought were white clouds in the blue sky. Our home state of Mecklenburg is flat as a pancake, and it wasn't until we got nearer that I realized that those white clouds were actually beautiful snow-topped mountains. I could not believe my eyes—and this was only the beginning!

After we gave our luggage to a porter, who spoke in an accent I did not understand, we slowly walked through a pretty, postcard-perfect village, and on the not-too-distant snow-covered slopes, I saw people on skis! I had never seen anybody on skis, and whenever I could get out of the hotel during the next two weeks I went as close as I could to the ski slopes and watched how those lucky people put on their skis and then literally flew down the mountain.

Another great experience of that trip happened just a few hours after our arrival—I met my first Roman Catholic!

At that time Northern Germany was almost 100 percent Evangelical Lutheran; Schwerin did not even have a functioning Catholic Church. I looked at my first Catholic person, namely Miss Erzenwald, the hotel manager, with the same wonder as I later looked at my first person of color and much later my first Asian.

After we were introduced in the little hotel office and I found out that Miss Erzenwald was actually a Catholic, I announced proudly, "I know a Catholic song!" My astonished mother said, "You do?" I was eleven years old and had never been to any church, except when I was baptized at six months of age or attended that one baptism of my cousin.

After my mother recovered from her shock, she said, "Let's hear it," and I sang the entire opening chorus from *Cavalleria Rusticana,* the opera by Mascagni.

As members of the children's ballet we had to appear on stage in crowd scenes, and I always raised my hand when volunteers were needed. My mother did not have the time to find out what I was doing, and both the housekeeper and my grandmother gave me all the freedom I needed. As long as I told them where I was going and was home after the theater was over, I was free as a bird.

In *Cavalleria* I had been a choirboy, waving my incense back and forth, and it had not taken many rehearsals and perfor-mances for me to memorize that chorus, one of the most beautiful choir pieces ever written.

Years later, when things got rough or we were very scared in an air-raid shelter, my mother used to say to me, "Sing me that Catholic song."

School Days

When we returned from Austria in the spring of 1938, I had changed. I had heard and maybe even understood the conspiratorial tone in which the new people my mother had met communicated. At first this fact only intrigued me, but then I wanted to know what was going on, and slowly and gently my mother told me that there were many people who were unwelcome to the Nazis. That there were those who actually dared to object to the Nazi rule, and these people either had to leave the country or were sent to concentration camps.

She told me that she and Miss Erzenwald and a few others were trying to help these people to leave Germany. The way she spoke to me was very loving and subtle. I was proud to be "in the know," and I don't recall that my mother ever told me not to tell anyone. It was just a secret I shared with her; however, it started to make me see and hear things differently.

At age twelve, school and my friends were an important part of my life. All schools in Germany were at that time strictly segregated, and even to this day, over seventy years later, none of my school friends or I could even imagine what it would have been like to go to school with the boys.

My mother had been the school physician to all-girls schools for six years before I ever started school. She knew all the teachers, and at the beginning of the school year she gave a physical examination to all first graders. That meant that she knew the pupils and very often their parents, too, and she had an incredible knack of spotting fanatical Nazis or their offspring after the first meeting.

There were few dangerous Nazis in our little northern town. A dangerous Nazi was one who would have been only too glad to report a Social Democrat, a homosexual, or someone who dared to say anything against the Nazi regime.

I did know quite a few girls, who were *Arbeiterkinder,* the daughters of blue color workers, because I met them on the way to school and we walked together. At that time, there was very little social integration in our town. Because of my mother's socialistic influence, I never gave these girls' social standing a second thought and invited them to all my often quite lavish birthday parties.

Even after all these years my best girl friend will say something like, "I could never understand what you saw in those common girls."

At school we used to sit in class and have to listen to our homeroom teacher, who gave us a synopsis of the Nazi version of the *Daily News* first thing in the morning. These daily reports were standard practice until our schools closed in January of 1945. We used to look at each other and roll our eyes. We were lucky, because most of our teachers did not believe the propaganda either.

After 1938 most of our teachers had to join the NSDAP or were automatically enrolled, sort of as a trade union. There was only one teacher whom we believed to be an actual Nazi, and not a very dangerous one at that.

Fräulein Kunert, whom we referred to as *"Die Kunertsche,"* wore the swastika pin on her blouse and had a little piece of extra material sown in the place where the pin went. That impressed us.

There are still ten of us classmates who keep in touch and meet whenever I'm in Europe, which lately has been annually. We actually still laugh about the little piece of material that reinforced that blouse for that Nazi pin. When I think of all the shared nightmares we could be talking about at those meetings, it is that little bit of material on Kunert's blouse that we laugh about.

Miss Kunert, who taught math and was good at it, was also the only teacher who actually raised her arm straight out for her Hitler salute as she entered the classroom. We would respond by lifting our behind from the chair, holding the back of the chair with our left hand, and making some sort of motion with our right hand while saying, *"Halben Lieter"* (Half a liter.), which, if you don't listen too closely, could pass for "Heil Hitler."

For the teachers we trusted, we got up properly, waved our right hand, and mumbled something unintelligible, sort of halfway between "halben Lieter" and *"guten Morgen."* When I hear how strict the Nazi indoctrination was in other parts of Germany, I am amazed. Berlin was only about two hundred miles away but it was in Brandenburg, Prussia—worlds away from Schwerin in Mecklenburg.

Starting when I was in third grade, I had private history lessons after school twice a week. The lessons were at the teacher's house, just a block away from the route I took on the way home from school. Even in those days, I knew what I could and could not say to anybody, even to my best and most trusted friends. I just waved my hand; said, *"Tschüss,"* the northern German version of "bye-bye"; and went on my way.

Many of us had private piano lessons or gymnastics after school, and fortunately, I was never questioned when I left the group walking home. To this day I find it difficult to lie; even the term *white lie* makes me uncomfortable, but I learned early in life that not saying anything is often a better solution.

My mother felt strongly that the history lessons I got in school were strictly Nazi propaganda, which indeed they were, and she wanted me to learn to distinguish fact from fiction.

Fräulein Schröder was my mother's patient and was devoted to her. As a high school history teacher, she suffered deeply by having to twist historical facts into Nazi lies in order to keep her job or even to prevent being sent to a concentration camp.

Quite often, we would see people listen at the classroom door or walk into the classroom unannounced to listen to the lecture. I was probably the only one in class who was disturbed by this.

I was nervous because of my father's background and also because of the things I had been told by my mother. Sometimes they were in full Nazi uniform, and sometimes they were not.

Such was school life under the Nazis.

I would report to Fräulein Schröder what I had been told in my third grade history class, and she kept me on the straight and narrow as far as the historical facts were concerned.

It was not always easy for me to keep the facts straight when I had to answer in school or when I reported to my mother and grandmother at home, but I seem to have managed.

Bless Fräulein Schröder. While my mother was wrapped up in her negative opinion of everything German, Fräulein Schröder was the one who assured me that although the German nation had totally gone astray for the time being, there was still a great deal of which I could be very proud. She spoke to me of the great German poets, the scientists whose discoveries of vaccines were saving lives all over the world, and the archaeologists, who did their work in Egypt, Greece, and South and Central America.

I see 1938 as the year in which I gave up, or rather lost, my childhood. For a little while I really thought that children who grew up in Nazi households were luckier, and I held that belief until the whole Nazi world started to collapse around us, just as my mother had predicted.

Those children had several years of believing that the German nation and the Aryan race were the greatest in the world and that they stood at the threshold of the "Thousand-Year Reich"; whereas I was only twelve years old, and I had to learn the facts and grow up with no illusions at all.

In retrospect, of course, I realize that I was the lucky one.

Sometime in 1938 I should have joined the Hitler Youth. When we got to high school—that was the fifth grade—the schools enrolled us automatically, and I probably am still on somebody's list. The Germans are frighteningly efficient, but either by incredibly good luck, which I doubt, or some very good connections, I fell through the cracks.

I never had a uniform and I never, ever attended a meeting. I was also never required to take part in any marches or those open-air assemblies. Hitler Youth just was not a big thing in our town and certainly not at our school. I don't ever remember seeing any girl wearing one of those ghastly, mustard brown jackets to school prior to a meeting, as we sometimes saw on girls from other schools.

I think that one of the reasons my status was never challenged was because I was so active and visible in the theater. The Nazis loved and supported their *kultur,* just as much as the Communists who followed them did. The bombs might be falling, the armies might be retreating, people might be wounded and starving, and the cities might be burning—but the theaters got new paint and new upholstery. Anybody employed by the theater got special housing and extra rations. That was a fact under the Nazis, just as it was later under the Communists.

Concentration Camps

Before we talk about Kristallnacht, that horrendous pogrom against the Jews on November 9, 1938, I want to talk briefly about the concentration camps, which were ready and waiting for the horrors to come.

Hitler and his cohorts did not wait long before they opened the first German concentration camp. The concept was not new; one only needs to look at history to find many examples of those shocking establishments.

The Nazis opened the first concentration camp in Dachau near Munich in March of 1933, less than two months after they came to power. They did this with great fanfare in the newspapers and on the *Wochenschau,* the newsreel that preceded every movie.

Concentration camps were called KZ, even when I think in English I use the harsh German pronunciation of those letters, which have become part of the German language—much like ESP and PBS are treated as words in American English.

The children in the schoolyard used to yell in play to each other, "Don't do that, or they'll put you in the KZ!" My mother had told me about these camps of horror, and I stood around while the schoolyard games went on and never said a word.

Even at that early age I had learned that it would be dangerous to tell anybody what my mother had told me.

To this day, it is a mystery to me how people could claim after the war and after all the horrors had been revealed that they had not ever heard of the concentration camps. It is a fact that the general public did not know about the mass executions, which did not start until 1942, and the extermination camps were not in Germany, but in Poland and the Ukraine. But everybody knew, or should have known, that there were concentration camps where thousands died from starvation, overwork, or as the result of medical experiments.

At first these camps were used as holding camps for "guest workers"—Jews from across Europe, Gypsies, ethnic Poles, soviet POWs, anti-Nazis, homosexuals, and any other people considered "undesirables." Even disabled Germans, those suffering from genetic diseases, and those who were crippled or mentally retarded were sent off to concentration camps.

The camps were also used as prisons for other criminals, such as black marketers. Criminals and homosexuals were sometimes released after they had served their time or when the concentration camps needed more space for newcomers.

Although those who were released were sworn to secrecy and threatened with immediate reimprisonment, the word about what was going on in there got out soon enough. The descriptions of the inhumane treatment, torture, malnutrition, ill health, gruesome medical experiments, and outright murder, which were all causes of death, were simply horrendous.

My mother heard about some of the cruel details from a relative.

Onkel Peter was sent to a concentration camp early under the Nazi regime, because he was a homosexual; he was released sometime in 1938. He was a physician just like my mother, and they knew each other well, because they had been in medical school together. After his release Peter had a brief visit with his mother and came to our house. I remember meeting him. He hugged me and said to my mother, "So, Anne Marie, you got what you always wanted, a daughter."

That made me happy, and I liked Onkel Peter from that moment on, but I would never see him again.

Peter and my mother drove off in her car. She often had to make house calls in the country, and I am sure they had taken a long walk in the forest after the patient visits, because my mother did not come home until hours later. When she did come home, she was alone.

Although I was only twelve years old at the time, I knew that she was badly shaken.

It was late, and she went straight to bed but asked me to join her. I sat by her bed until well after midnight and listened to what my mother felt I needed to know as the child and confidant of a Resistance worker. She explained homosexuality to me in such a loving and understanding way that I was neither upset nor disgusted. That night, she laid the cornerstone for the incredible trust I had in her and also for my lifelong tolerance of all people, no matter their race or lifestyle.

In Germany, at least at that time, the article in the German *Reichsgesetz,* the federal law making homosexuality illegal, was paragraph 175; therefore, all homosexuals, male and female, were referred to as *Hundert-Fünfundsiebziger* (one hundred seventy-fivers).

That is the only name we ever knew, and I had to learn the current and politically correct names years later when I returned to Germany.

Although I was never shocked at the things my mother said to me, I did have a hard time when she told me about the medical experiments Onkel Peter had to perform. He must have gone into great detail on that long walk they took in the forest.

Most medical experiments were designed to help the German army. There were experiments of long exposure to extreme cold or heat, submerging human beings under water to nearly the point of drowning, and injecting people with bacteria to measure how soon their temperature rose and to see at which point they could recover or their kidneys would be destroyed.

Typically, these experiments resulted in death, trauma, disfigurement, or permanent disability, and they must be considered, to this day, as medical torture.

I was filled with shock and sadness when my mother finished, and how I managed to crawl into my cozy bed, get some sort of a good night's sleep, and meet my friends the next morning at school and never say a single thing about this is a mystery to me.

Other parents should have had similar stories to tell their children, but they probably never did.

I do understand that what was happening in the concentrations camps before the war would not exactly have been dinner conversation in front of children, just as I do not believe that the goings on at Guantanamo Bay and Abu Ghraib are the subject of discussion in American households in front of children. But any adult who lived in Germany during the thirties who claims not to have known about the concentration camps is just plain lying or lived under a rock somewhere.

One interesting fact here.

After the war, military governments, and later the German government, too, gave certain privileges to concentration camp victims, such as extra ration cards, housing, and preferred exit visas. And so it should be. But apparently they never asked why anyone had been in a concentration camp, so black marketers and smugglers got the same privileges as Jews and other persecuted people who had survived.

I met the wife of a black marketer in Greece, and she bragged about how clever he had been to get out of Germany so easily after the war.

An important point is that Himmler and his cohorts did not come up with the Final Solution until 1941, when Jewish people were brought into Germany on forced transports by the thousands and the camps simply ran out of space. The extermination camps, especially the one at Auschwitz in Poland, could "process" a trainload of one thousand living human beings in one hour, ten thousand per day. They did not start those horrendous operations until early 1942.

Security being what it was during the war in Germany, the lack of personal travel and communication and the fact that there were no survivors from the extermination camps make it believable that the German people did not know in its entirety what was happening.

Even my mother, who really had her ears close to the ground, knew only that many, many Jews and others were murdered. Even she did not know the extent or the methods of the bestiality until concentration camp survivors started to drift into our town.

Onkel Peter was not heard from again until after the war. He had gone straight into the army as a military doctor and after the war opened a successful medical practice in West Germany. My mother visited him there once or twice. Several nieces and nephews who had fled to the West came to stay with him in later years. He and his housekeeper cared for them, and he put some of them through medical and dental school.

Onkel Peter is fondly remembered even to this day.

Kristallnacht

November 9, 1938.

I had just turned twelve in September, and after hearing all the reports of what happened during the night of November 9 and on November 10, I was no longer a child.

There had been a vague feeling of unease in the air for several days, a kind of inexplicable saber rattling. Maybe I noticed it only because I was making some modest preparations for my mother's birthday, which was on November 9.

She kept saying, "Don't do anything, I am far too busy. I might be called away."

As it turned out, all I did was go to the local bookstore, where I was well known, to buy a nice folder of copies of Dürer woodcuts and charge it to her account. Although I never saw her look at that Dürer collection, she must have treasured it, because when I went through her things after she died in 1981, I found it with the few things she had been able to get out of the Russian Zone.

As I think about it, November 9 has been a fateful day in both my family and German history. My Onkel Anton crashed and perished in his sabotaged plane on November 9 in World War I. November 9, 1923, marked Hitler's failed *Putsch* (coup attempt), after which he went to jail and wrote *Mein Kampf.* We managed to get through all the Nazi years without letting a copy of that book into our house. Amazingly enough, it was never required reading in our school, and I have no intention of ever reading it.

Many years later, the Berlin Wall fell on November 9, 1989. How I wish that my mother had still been alive to see East Germans breaking through that wall and being received with open arms on the other side.

Now it was 1938, and I went to bed in my lovely room way upstairs under the roof. My mother's bedroom was directly underneath mine, and I heard the phone ring several times during the night, and I heard voices and my mother going in and out.

The next morning I was told that the office of Dr. Rosenbaum, who practiced medicine around the corner, had been destroyed, and he had been taken away. My mother had forewarned him, and he had wisely sent his family away. My mother took care of all his patients after that, and she never charged them a thing. Some people insisted on paying, and she kept that money in a separate account, which was closed by the Russian occupation.

The Rosenbaums never came back.

I heard that the store windows in the two jewelry stores and several clothing stores that were owned by Jews had been smashed and that the owners and their families had disappeared. Those stores had been there for years, and now people were sweeping up the broken glass.

Our town was a quiet town of about fifty-two thousand inhabitants and was so rural that people often kidded that Schwerin had not quite entered the twentieth century yet. Everybody knew everybody, and the few Jews in town were totally absorbed by the community. The very idea that such a horror could be committed by our own people against those who were our neighbors and whom we passed every day in the street was overwhelming, disgusting, and immensely frightening.

A few days after Kristallnacht we got a letter from Minna Eberson, who had been housekeeper to my grandaunt and godmother for many years. After Tante Lotte moved into a retirement home, Minna had taken a position in a Jewish household in Osnabrück. Both Tante Lotte and my mother always felt that Minna really *belonged* to our family, and my mother had promised her that she would hire Minna as soon as she was financially able to support a full-time housekeeper.

Minna's letter was a cry for help.

After Kristallnacht, when her employer and his wife were taken away and the household was totally destroyed, Minna walked all night to her brother's house, who took loving care of her. She found my mother's address, and her brother encouraged her to write a letter to us.

Needless to say, my mother immediately sent money for the train fare from Osnabrück in Western Germany to Schwerin, and a few days later Minna arrived at our house, practically without luggage. She got the room next to mine.

Minna remained our faithful housekeeper until Schwerin was occupied by the Russians in July of 1945. It was from her that I heard some of the gruesome and personal details of what really happened during Kristallnacht.

After Minna went to her room on her second night at our house, my mother said to me, "Go and talk to Minna." I gently knocked at her door and heard a tiny, tearful voice saying, *"Herein."* (Come in.) I found Minna sitting up on her bed, still fully dressed, with her eyes closed and her knees drawn up to her chest, gently rocking back and forth.

Though I was only twelve years old, I sensed that when my mother told me to talk to Minna, she had really meant, "Go and listen to Minna."

I pulled up a chair close to Minna's bed and just sat there with my legs crossed under me, tailor fashion, and waited. After a little while she started to talk. Her eyes were still closed, and tears were running down her cheeks.

Here is what she told me:

The Glaubachs, her employers, lived in a beautiful upstairs apartment in one of the nicest parts of Osnabrück in Westphalia. On November 9 at around 11:00 p.m., someone pounded on the front door and Mr. Glaubach, who was about seventy years old, put on his robe and opened the door. There was some yelling, and Minna slipped on her robe and joined Mr. and Mrs. Glaubach in the hall. There were three men, one in full Nazi uniform and two in civilian clothes, one carrying a sledgehammer and the other one an ax, and they looked eager to make use of those tools.

The man in uniform grabbed the Glaubachs and pushed them onto two chairs, stood between them holding them each by the shoulders, and said, "Now watch and see what we think of you shit-Jews." Then he ordered the two men to get on with it. The two hoodlums smashed everything in the apartment—the furniture, the lamps, even the kitchen appliances. After breaking all of the windowpanes they threw the precious china, the silver, and the ornaments out of the windows. They had special fun with the chandelier, breaking as many of the precious crystal pieces as they could reach and letting out a big yell with the breaking of every lightbulb.

When it was dark in the apartment, the man in the uniform grabbed Mr. and Mrs. Glaubach and said something like, "Out with you." When Mr. Glaubach, who was a severe diabetic, asked whether he could take his insulin, he was told, "You won't need it."

Minna listened as the Glaubachs were dragged down the stairs, and she stood in the pitch-dark apartment paralyzed with fear. The hoodlums had direct orders not to damage the property of, and not to hurt, anybody who was not a Jew. But Minna could not know that as she crept out of the apartment and, dressed only in her robe and slippers on a cold November night, started on the long walk through the center of town to the house of her brother.

She did not tell me much about that walk, did not mention the burning synagogues, the injured and dying people on the side-walk, the crying women, and the silent children. I knew about all that from my mother, since it had happened in all major German cities and word got around very fast.

Within a short while my mother got some statistics, which are well known today. All over Germany the glass storefronts of 7,500 Jewish stores and businesses where smashed, hence the name *Kristallnacht* (Crystal Night). Over 1,500 synagogues were torched or destroyed, and over thirty thousand men were taken to concentration camps.

The treatment in the concentration camps was brutal, but after a few months the men and their families were given permission to leave Germany provided they could pay for the journey and would leave all of their property and investments behind.

Minna never ever got over the Kristallnacht experience, and since it helped her to talk about it and since we were not allowed to say anything aloud about what happened, I sat by her bedside for many evenings to come.

She became and always remained our true friend and confidant, and I have often wondered how much she actually knew about my mother's—and later my—activities in the Resistance move-ment, which after Kristallnacht became so much larger a part of our lives.

The Invasion of Poland

There were always rumors that Hitler would start a war. At least in our house there was always that cloud hanging over our heads. It was difficult to get real news. The airwaves and newspapers were under the control of the Nazis, and it was difficult and strictly forbidden to listen to any foreign broadcasts. There was a red sticker on every radio, listing the forbidden wavelengths. If you listened anyway and then talked about it, or if the broadcast was overheard by a neighbor or passerby, the offense was punishable by death.

My uncle Andre, who was an opera singer in Bern, Switzerland, would write to tell us when he would be on the radio, but try as we may, we never really got to hear him. There was always interference, which was so loud that we could only hear an occasional note.

Even the best Blaupunkt radio could not overcome the Nazi interference, and my grandmother was heartbroken.

I had never heard my uncle sing because in those days, in 1934 and 1935, we did not even own a gramophone. Anyway, I doubt that there were even any gramophone records of my uncle singing arias. At age seven I did not know what I was missing, but seeing my grandmother cry and clutch our radio broke my heart. All letters coming in from abroad were opened, and every telegram message was censored. Getting any kind of travel visa was almost impossible.

My grandmother visited my uncle in Switzerland once in 1934 and then never again. She brought back an enlarged photograph of the three mountains overlooking the little town of Bern— Eiger, Mönch (Monk) and Jungfrau (Virgin). Jungfrau got its name because there is always a cloud around the mountain- top, like a bridal veil. I heard a great deal about those moun- tains, and in 1975 when I traveled with my teenage daughter in Switzerland, I was able to show her the Virgin Mountain with the bridal veil.

Onkel Andre visited us once in 1936 when travel was a little easier because of the upcoming Olympic Games, but I don't remember whether he sang for us during that visit. Surely he must have sung for us, but all I remember is that he talked to my mother and my grandmother for a long time and told them that it was a well-known fact in Switzerland that Hitler was planning a war.

In Switzerland they talked about that quite openly, and my uncle was shocked by the fact that in Germany the people were either in complete denial or too afraid to talk.

That kind of conversation really scared me, and I hoped that it was not true. Both my uncle and his wife, who was also an opera singer, had to leave Switzerland in 1938 because Germans were becoming persona non grata and would most certainly not be engaged by any opera house.

The war started on September 1, 1939, with Germany's invasion of Poland.

Two days later, England and France declared war on Germany.

Both England and France had entered into a treaty with Poland earlier in the year when it was no longer a secret that Hitler was on the warpath. They had promised to help protect the German-Polish border in case of an attack.

Unfortunately, and to their shame, all they did was to declare war on Hitler's Germany and then never did a single thing to help Poland. Most Germans did not know about that treaty, but my mother knew, and she never forgave Great Britain and France for their neglect. The world would have been a different place, at least for a little while.

The nightmare had started, and it would last for six years.

The people of Mecklenburg were appalled by the invasion of Poland. That country had been divided many times, and many people there were German speaking. The big landowners, of which my grandfather had been one, were interrelated with the landowners of East Prussia, Latvia, Estonia, and Lithuania.

The German press made no secret of the fact that the army was transporting workers from the occupied countries and putting them into holding or labor camps. These horror camps had a big sign over each gate, reading, *"Arbeit macht frei"* (work makes free).

Since there was a real labor shortage in Germany as soon as the war started, this move was acceptable to some people. My mother never let me forget how very wrong this was, and that it was imported slave labor.

Right from the beginning of the war, every able-bodied man was conscripted into the armed forces or otherwise employed in the war effort. The women worked the land or in stores and offices in addition to having the honor and duty of keeping the home front together, which included to keep on having children. We heard a lot about that.

The war with Poland lasted thirty-six days, and many of the soldiers were given leave for the winter. Hitler was planning his attacks on the rest of Europe for the early spring of 1940.

Some of those soldiers were my mother's patients and made office appointments with her because they felt physically ill. Post-traumatic stress disorder did not originate with the war in Iraq!

As soon as my mother realized that a soldier wanted to talk about his experience in Poland, she would suggest a walk in the garden; that is where she heard the unbelievable horror stories that she shared with me daily in our special little room.

The Nazis had nothing but contempt for the Slavic races, and they made this known at every possible opportunity. They considered them subhuman, along with Jews, Roma (Gypsies), and Negroes. When I asked about the Asiatic races—because even at thirteen I could see the inconsistency—my mother smiled a sad smile and said, "We can't say anything against the Japanese, because the Japanese are our allies."

The Polish campaign was an instance of total war, and right from the beginning the *Luftwaffe* (German air force) bombed cities and villages mercilessly and attacked the fleeing population from the air. The soldiers were ordered to burn all villages to the ground and shoot every man, woman, and child, as well as the dogs.

At the beginning of the war, Hitler's SS, the Schutzstaffel, was divided into three groups—the General SS, which concerned itself with police and racial matters; the Armed SS, which consisted of combat troops within the Nazi military; and the SS death's-head squad, which ran the concentration and extermination camps.

Of course, none of these black-uniformed devils would have come to speak to my mother, but the young, inexperienced soldiers came to talk to her and told her what they could not even tell their parents.

My mother heard how they had to watch as hundreds of Jews, Gypsies, and members of the Polish elite were forced to dig their own graves. They were then shot from behind so that they would fall right into the ditches without having to be moved. The soldiers had to fill the ditches, shooting any victim who was still moving, while the SS walked away.

How my mother could stand to listen to all this and then continue with her normal office hours has always remained a mystery to me, and maybe she told me so much of this—the only person in the world she could really trust—because she simply had to tell someone.

It was many, many years later that I looked up the statistics of the invasion and occupation of Poland and found out about Operation *Tannenberg*. This was a code name for an organization that, with the help of a small German minority living in Poland, established a list that would identify over sixty-one thousand members of the Polish elite: activists, intelligentsia, scholars, actors, former officers, and others who were to be interned or shot.

Apart from the tremendous losses of life due to air raids and battles in September 1939, during Operation Tannenberg in the same month, twenty thousand civilians were shot at 760 execution sites. Of course, we did not know those numbers, but we knew about the horrors, and until the end of the war I lived my teenage years under a cloud of secrecy and fear.

Refugees and Getting the News

The war went on and on.

Between April and June 1940, Germany invaded Denmark and Norway and attacked Western Europe. Luxemburg, the Netherlands, and Belgium surrendered in May, and France signed the armistice on June 22. Germany occupied the entire North Sea and Atlantic coast and the northern part of France. Every morning in school we had to follow the victories of the German army in great detail on a huge map, and my girlfriends and I just sat there and rolled our eyes at each other. The fathers of these girls were high-ranking officers, and I know that the information they got at home was quite different from the propaganda we were fed at school.

After the surrender of France, the Germans tried to establish total control of the airspace above all of Europe. The only thing in their way was the RAF, Britain's Royal Air Force.

In August of 1940, the Luftwaffe attacked all radar installations and air bases in Britain, and although they did considerable damage, they were thoroughly defeated in air battles during the *Battle of Britain* in July through October of 1940.

As a result, Hitler abandoned his planned and much feared invasion of the British Isles. It is surprising, but in spite of all our good connections we never did hear about that, or at least, nobody ever talked about it, and I have to confess that I never heard the term the *Battle of Britain* until 1946, after I had emigrated to England.

On June 22, 1942, the Nazis began their invasion of the Soviet Union, which was Germany's former ally. Many Germans were disgusted by that, and at that point we started to hear whispered comments that Russia had been Napoleon's downfall and that this was the beginning of the end for Germany. We did not have to listen any longer to our schoolteachers or the rumormongers on how the war was going, because now we got our information firsthand from the people who were fleeing from the battle zone.

I saw my first refugees at the end of 1942 when I was sixteen, when desperate people came from Poland, East Prussia, and the Baltic States, frantically trying to find safety in Germany and the western countries. The faces of those haunted, homeless, cold, and hungry people will remain in my memory for the rest of my life. They had to leave their homes, and everything they knew and loved, behind. Some came by train, but most of them were walking, pushing their few belongings on bicycles and in baby buggies and pulling their toddlers in small wagons packed in pillows.

It was a natural though never discussed fact that the residents of our town and in all of Mecklenburg opened their doors and offered them food and shelter. Many of the refugees stayed for only a few days unless they had relatives in the area, but most of them wanted to move as far west as possible.

I did not sleep in my own room after the fall of 1942; it was always occupied by refugees, who sometimes changed on a daily basis. My bed was moved into my mother's bedroom, which yielded a double benefit, making my room available for refugees and making it much easier for me to answer the phone for my mother all night. In those days there was no such thing as a physician's telephone exchange, and a doctor had to answer his (or her) own phone at night. When I was in my mother's bedroom, I had the phone on my bedside table so she could get a few hours of sleep.

I got very good at sorting out which calls were from real patients needing help and which calls came from her Resistance connections. I always woke her for the calls from people connected with the Resistance. The caller would hang up unless I said, "Just a moment, I'll get my mother." Even after they knew my voice, I could sense that they were uncomfortable speaking to me.

In July of 1943, the catastrophic firebombing of Hamburg occurred, where forty-three thousand civilians were literally burned to death and almost a million people had to leave their devastated city.

The towns and villages of Mecklenburg sent as many trucks and cars as they could muster to the outskirts of Hamburg—my mother in her small car included—and they picked up as many air-raid victims as their vehicles could possibly hold.

During July, we had seven air-raid victims from Hamburg in our house—one couple and five women. Two of the women were badly burned on their hands and faces, and everybody's burned and singed clothes were hanging in shreds from their bodies. These people had been through hell, and to my horror I could see and smell it. The refugees slept either in my room or on the floor in the loft, and all the women shared our kitchen and our food.

Most of the refugees, whether they were from Poland, the Soviet Union, the Baltic States, or Hamburg, were in a state of shock and spoke very little—not to each other, and most certainly not to us. However, there were always one or two who would sit with my mother late at night, glad to have found an understanding and trustworthy woman, and they would tell her their sad and frightening stories. I often sat in on those conversations and gained a lot of insight not really suitable for a sixteen-year-old. I was deeply moved and always frightened.

It was a good thing that I now had a new source of information and spent most of my evenings, and often half the night, under the covers of my bed listening to the BBC, the famous British Broadcasting Corporation. Yes, by the end of 1942 the BBC had finally broken its way through the German interference, and my mother had managed to get me a strictly forbidden shortwave radio.

After listening for a while, I began to recognize the voices of the reporters, and thanks to the excellent quality of the radio, most of the news came through unscrambled.

I particularly liked the reports that always started with, *"Jetzt hören Sie die Stimme eines deutschen Offiziers"* (now you hear the voice of a German officer).

Deep down in my heart I did not really like the idea of a German officer, whom I felt must have been a deserter, broadcasting from England, but his reports were excellent, addressing the German people not as monsters but as human beings. The hardest thing about listening to the BBC was to keep quiet about it. It was dangerous to spread BBC information. It was yet another crime that was punishable by death.

In that connection, I have a wonderful story—not the death, but the listening.

After I came to England in 1946, I had to finish my high school and prepare for my college entrance examination. All of our final examinations were held at King's College in Newcastle upon Tyne, and I went there by train every day for an entire week in June 1947.

As a special favor I was allowed to take German as one of my foreign language requirements. The teachers were really nice and said that since I was doing everything else, including French, in what was to me a foreign language (namely, English), I deserved a break.

Since I was understandably the only student taking a German oral examination, I was taken into the professor's office. Casually, and maybe even disinterestedly, he handed me a newspaper and said, "Read anything you want." I got the feeling that he thought he had me because the paper was printed in Gothic script, but that was no problem for me, and I just started to read.

After barely two sentences he said, "Stop. And what part of northern Germany did you come from?" When I told him I came from Schwerin in Mecklenburg, he asked whether I had spent the war in Germany. When I answered yes, he asked, "Did you ever listen to the BBC?" I nodded my head, and at that moment his voice and whole expression changed as he said, "Jetzt hören Sie die Stimme eines deutschen Offiziers."

I was completely stunned and yelled, "I know you, I know you!" and almost jumped across the desk to him.

That was an incredible moment, I think for both of us— a moment I shall never forget for as long as I live. Of course, the examination ended right there, and he asked me to the next college function at King's College so that I could meet his wife, who had sat by him during so many of his broadcasts.

To return to the war: It was in the evening of December 11, 1941, a Thursday, that I was walking home from the opera house after a rehearsal. As usual, it was very dark, and if I had not known our little town so well, it could have been frightening. We all wore little pins on our coats, which gave off a greenish fluorescence. You could get them in the shape of a circle or a heart, and I always wore a heart.

Just as I was crossing the market square, the public loudspeaker started to blare, letting us know that there would be a special announcement by the *Oberkommando der Wehrmacht,* the High

Command of the Armed Forces, and we all stopped in our tracks.

The announcement told us that Germany had declared war on the United States of America in support of our glorious allies, the Japanese.

You can be assured that there was not a single person in that square who gave a darn about the Japanese, and most people did not even know that they were supposed to be our glorious allies. The announcement was repeated twice. You could have cut the silence with a knife at that moment on that little market square in Schwerin.

There was no explanation, nothing about Pearl Harbor—where, when, or what it was—and to all of us it was just another inexplicable decision by our Führer, who, after the invasion of the Soviet Union in the summer of 1941, was seen by an ever larger number of Germans as a megalomaniac.

People were much too afraid to talk about it aloud, but there were whispers, and more and more of them dared to whisper to us—my mother and me—because we were so openly anti-Nazi.

I dashed home and without much of an explanation and without taking off my clothes jumped into bed, pulled the covers over my head, and waited for my friend the German officer to tell me over the shortwave exactly what had happened. Oh, what I would have given in those days to know that the German officer was not a deserter but a German professor at King's College in Newcastle upon Tyne.

It was hard for me to figure out what really happened at Pearl Harbor, and it did not become clear to me until I visited Pearl Harbor many years later, but I did understand that America had entered the war. When I told my mother that Hitler had declared war on America, she hugged me tight and said, "Thank God, thank God; now the madness will end."

But the madness went on for another three and a half years.

Zwetschgen Strudel

My mother had made her Austrian connection in the spring of 1938, when Austria became a part of the Reich, the German empire. She kept in contact through couriers, who could still travel within Germany, and we had traveled to Innsbruck and Seefeld in Tirol every spring and summer until the fall of 1941, when my mother could no longer leave Schwerin and her medical practice.

Most local physicians were somewhere on the battlefields with the armed forces, and she took over the patients from as many of them as she possibly could.

Of course, as she was the only doctor in Schwerin who stubbornly refused to join the Nazi party, people who were insured with the National Health System were not supposed to be treated by her, but she solved the problem by simply not charging them, and they all loved being her patients.

The *Ärztekammer,* the medical association, which had become a Nazi organization in the thirties, was furious with her, but really, with the shortage of physicians and her great popularity in this

small town, there was not much they could do about her successful practice.

As far as the Austrian connection was concerned, I took over
where my mother left off. At fifteen I was mature for my age
and maybe, because of the way things had happened, I missed
the teenage part of my life, but I was still young and fearless
enough to want to be actively involved.

Nobody in my circle of friends got the chance to travel to
Innsbruck and Vienna at least three times a year, and I had an
opportunity to do that in spite of the war, in spite of the school
I missed, and in spite of the personal travel restrictions imposed
by the Nazis.

My mother managed it all. I have no idea what she told the
school principal, how she got the travel permits, or how she
coped with the fear that the train would be bombed or that some
SS bully might stop me and find the hidden papers in my suitcase. Once, I was stopped by two of those black beasts, as I
called them in my mind, as I was changing trains in Munich.

"Hey there, where do you come from, and where are you going?"
they asked in their rough and arrogant voices.

I thought that they must surely hear my loudly pounding heart.
"I came from Schwerin, and I am going to Vienna."

"Show your papers, and what is your reason for traveling?"

Fortunately, I had an identity card, showing that I was a resident
of Schwerin and attended the local lyceum, which was what

a high school for girls was called at that time. Shrugging my shoulders as if the whole thing was not important, I told them that I just had to get away from all the bombing for a little while. That answer spontaneously popped into my head, and I had a narrow escape, because if they had been just a little bit smarter or a little better trained, they would have known that Schwerin was in Mecklenburg, which had not been bombed in years, and that school girls did not travel all across Germany to Austria to get away from any bombing.

They told me to go on. One of the guys in black with the skull on his shoulders winked obscenely, and the other clicked his tongue, and I was on my way.

That is about all I remember about that particular trip, but the memory of my last trip to Vienna in the spring of 1944 is still vivid in my mind. Maybe it is still such an important part of my memory because it was my last trip, and actually the last time I saw my beloved Vienna.

Vienna, with its fabulous *Ringstrasse,* museums, opera house, *Stephansdom* (St. Stephen's Cathedral, which I climbed time and again), *Prater* (Vienna's amusement park with its giant ferris wheel), and all those bridges across the not-so-blue Danube. Vienna, where I had a spring in my step like nowhere else and I thought that there was the music of a waltz by Strauss coming out of every café. With all my trips to Europe after leaving Germany, I have just never had the heart to go back.

In 1944, Germany and the rest of Europe had been at war for five years, and things were going badly for the Germans. But to say so was yet another offense punishable by death. What I was doing, carrying secret papers for the underground, was punishable by death, too, but there was so much dying all around, you somehow got numb to it.

My last trip turned out to be an especially hard journey. In Berlin I climbed into the most overcrowded train imaginable and secured a tiny corner in the passage outside the compartments. There was just room enough for me to sit on my small suitcase as long as I clasped my hands tightly around my knees, hoping that nobody would step on my feet.

People, mostly refugees and soldiers, stood or crouched around me. I could not see a window, which did not matter too much since it was pitch black outside, and for a little while I could not even see the dimly lit ceiling of that supposedly first class railroad car. Fortunately, the soldier who really had me wedged in took off his huge backpack, squeezed it next to me, and sat down.

The train rattled into the night, now without any lights, and its silent passengers tried to preserve as much of their human dignity as was possible under the circumstances. Nobody could move even an inch. We shared what little food we had, and for the very desperate, the soldiers passed their steel helmets and emptied them out the window. I wondered what my mother would have said if she could have seen me on this journey, which she had arranged, and which would hopefully save one or two lives.

The train trip from Berlin to Vienna took a little under twelve hours. All carriages were securely locked as we passed into Czechoslovakia and silently rolled through Prague, one of the most beautiful cities of Europe.

The guards unlocked every carriage separately as we crossed the border into Austria.

Daylight had broken. The people at the window announced that we had crossed the Danube. Yes, the bridge was still there, and a little while later our train came to a screeching halt at the *Nordbahnhof*, Vienna's North Station.

Slowly, very, very slowly, the exhausted passengers got off the train. Even I, only seventeen years old, thought that my knees would buckle after twelve hours in that crouched position.

All was well when I spotted Tante Kristel, my mother's friend and her Resistance connection in Vienna. She was anxiously surveying the tired crowd and opened her arms wide when she saw me. Her tight, secure embrace felt so good.

I had been my mother's courier for over two years by then, when telephone and telegraph were diligently watched over by the *Gestapo* (the feared German state secret police), and my trips had taken me to Innsbruck and Vienna. It is surprising that I never seriously thought about the fact that I was carrying secret, important messages in that suitcase of mine.

As soon as we arrived at the apartment, Kristel and her husband (one of the leading internists in Vienna, if not in Europe) took my suitcase, and Bepperl, their housekeeper, gave me a big hug and sent me off to the bathroom. There was a soft bathrobe and the most marvelous-smelling soap provided just for me. After I cleaned up I went to Bepperl's kitchen, barefoot and wearing only that incredibly cozy bathrobe.

Bepperl was a live-in housekeeper. Her bedroom was next to the kitchen, and she had transformed a corner of the kitchen into her living room. There was a small bookshelf, a sewing box, a reading lamp, and one of those chairs that, once you have sunk into it, you never wanted to get out of again.

Tired as I was, I could not fall into that chair yet, because Bepperl said, "I have the dough resting, but you can help me with the *zwetschgen,*" and brought out a whole basket of those little, slightly sour Austrian plums. They are not particularly good for eating but are really quite wonderful for baking, especially in *Strudel.*

We halved the plums, took out the pits, and quartered them. Bepperl put them all in a bowl and mixed them with lots of sugar (to my great relief), chopped nuts (I have no idea how they got nuts in Austria; in Germany we had not had any nuts for years), then lots of dry breadcrumbs to absorb the juice.

Finally came the time to work on the dough, and I could sink into that wonderful chair.

Instead of falling asleep, I watched Bepperl with fascination as she worked the dough on a table that was about thirty-six inches square and covered with a white cloth. She rolled the dough into a circle and put it in the center of the table. Then she performed the most amazing acrobatics with that dough. She pulled it and rolled it, stuck her fist under it and lifted it so that it hung over her fist like a collapsed umbrella, pulled it, whirled it around, and threw it back on the table, only to roll it and pull it again. I could not believe my tired and droopy eyes.

All the time she kept up a constant stream of conversation about her wonderful nephew, Hansl, who was an officer and driving a tank in Italy, and how handsome he was, and how he was coming on leave to Vienna this very week, and would I not like to meet him, and on and on.

By that time, my head was rolling back and I could barely watch as Bepperl put the plums on the dough, drizzled some butter on it, and rolled it all up.

I don't remember too much after that except smelling an incredibly sweet scent in the kitchen and feeling that I was warm and cozy and safe. I woke only once to the noise of Bepperl opening the oven door to brush more butter on her strudel. The smell intensified and mixed with the smell of browning butter—and then I was fast asleep.

Later, I found out that, exhausted as I was, Bepperl was keeping me in the kitchen while Kristel quite literally was taking my small suitcase apart to get the top secret papers I was carrying for the Resistance. Although I knew I was carrying secret documents, both my mother and Kristel had decided that it was safer for me if I did not know exactly where they were.

In later years, people have asked me whether I did not feel any resentment against my mother and those who were taking advantage of me and my youth. I can quite honestly say that the thought never even occurred to me. I was proud to be part of this very important work. During that time, all of us were always in danger of our lives, and if I could do just one tiny bit to make it better for someone, I was ready and willing to do so.

The Battle of the Bulge

While the newspapers and the radio broadcasts were telling us about "Strategic realignments of the undefeatable German army," all around us it was getting colder and darker as we approached the Christmas season of 1944. Food rations were cut almost weekly, and all coal deliveries were stopped. Most people, especially the refugees, were constantly cold and hungry, and there was an unspoken fear of the Allied forces, particularly the Soviet army, coming closer and closer.

Refugees from the eastern front sat in total silence or told such horror stories that the only kindness I could give them was to sit and listen when I had the time. Our schools were closed in the middle of December, supposedly for the Christmas holidays, but a week later we were informed that, due to a shortage of coal, they would not reopen until the spring.

Sometime in early December I answered a ring at our front door, and there stood a young German army officer in a badly torn and dirty uniform. From what was left of his shoulder lapels I could see that he was an *Oberleutnant* (lieutenant first class). He said that his name was Kurt Eberson and that he was our housekeeper, Minna's, nephew. He had walked and hitched rides with army vehicles all the way from the eastern front somewhere in Poland, and he said that he was going to walk home to Hanover in Westphalia.

As we climbed the three long flights of stairs to Minna's room, I noticed that his left knee was stiff and apparently very painful. I helped him remove what was left of his jacket and his boots, which obviously had not been off his feet for a long time, and told him to lie on the bed and that I would call Minna. When I told her who was upstairs on her bed, she let out a scream, left whatever she was doing in the kitchen, and ran upstairs.

The house was full of refugees, and during office hours and even beyond those hours at least fifteen to twenty patients were sitting in the waiting room and on the stairs leading to our apartments. It was not easy to contact my mother during the day without being overheard.

I somehow got to her and managed to tell her about Kurt in Minna's room, and she went up to check on him and Minna as soon as she was able.

We were always short of beds and blankets, but my mother reassured me that Minna had it all under control. Kurt was sleeping in her bed and she would be sleeping on the floor, and in between all her other chores she would take care of him, nurse him, and bring him his food.

With so many people all around, I soon forgot about Kurt and went on with my busy life. I helped my mother during her long office hours, especially after the nurse and the office secretary had gone home in the afternoon. Until that time, our staff slept in our house and went home only on weekends, but with all the refugees in our house, my mother encouraged everyone to go home for the night whenever possible.

Minna was from Osnabrück, and at that time Westphalia was worlds away—besides, she was also a member of the family and would always stay with us.

When I was not helping in the office, I visited patients. I brought them their medications and often some food, and I changed dressings when necessary—my mother had many patients with open sores. When I finished all that work, I answered the phone for her all night.

Schwerin had been spared the day and night bombing by both the British and the Americans, and our little town was practically undestroyed. Therefore, at the end of December 1944 Schwerin was declared a *Lazarettstadt,* a town of army hospitals under the protection of the Red Cross.

This took effect January 1, 1945. The declaration meant that all schools, dance halls, and military barracks were converted into army hospitals. The opera house had already been closed in September of 1944 with a performance of Beethoven's *Fidelio,* and all cinemas were closed in December to provide more shelter for the hundreds of refugees.

The frantic preparations of converting schools and dance halls into hospitals began just before Christmas, and my mother was quite involved. She called on her friends from the local pharmacy to stock the army hospitals with as many medications and other medical supplies as were still available after five years of war.

High school students and very old men became carpenters and built bunk beds. The military set up a field kitchen in every hospital, and I do not know how they got mattresses, pillows and blankets, pots and pans, plates and cups, and all the other necessary things to run a hospital, however primitive.

It was a cold winter, and there was no coal for the central heating, but I do not remember a single soldier complaining about an uncomfortable bed or even of being cold. They had been through so much, and there were so many other things to worry about, that being cold and physically uncomfortable became a way of life for all of us.

One evening, Kurt, whom I had almost forgotten, knocked on our living room door—the only room that was truly our own. The refugees and patients respected our privacy, but as Minna's nephew, Kurt was family, and he was treated as such. I had not heard him come down the stairs, and that maneuver must have been difficult for him, considering the stiff knee. He was in his stocking feet. I know that this is hard to understand these days, but he had been well brought up, and for a German officer to walk around without shoes, especially when there were ladies present, was unthinkable.

Kurt immediately apologized and explained that Minna had mended his socks but had taken his boots to the shoemaker. The shoemaker, after soling our shoes with some synthetic stuff that was about as useful as cardboard, had found some actual leather for the boots.

When I picked up those boots our shoemaker said, "These good soles are for our soldier, who fought for us and is now walking home."

To this day I am still quite touched by those words.

Kurt asked if we had a newspaper in the house. Because of his long walk from the front and his convalescence, he did not have any idea what was happening on the eastern front and in the west.

I explained to him that to the best of my knowledge, no newspaper had been published all month, and we got our information directly from refugees and rumors. Then I whispered to him, "There is a shortwave radio in my bed."

His face lit up as he looked at me unbelievingly. To own a shortwave radio was everybody's dream, and now we had to find a way to get it out of my bed and put it in a place where we could both safely listen. When the coast was clear, we went into my mother's bedroom, got the radio out of my bed, and brought it into the living room. After some discussion, we decided that the space under my mother's writing desk would be the safest, because we could hide the radio behind the wastebasket and the sides of the desk would baffle the sound.

Kurt got down on the floor and started tuning the radio. At first he went to the one and only German station, and to our astonishment we heard that the German army, on the direction of Adolf Hitler, had started its counterattack in the west, called *Unternehmen Wacht am Rhein* (Operation Watch on the Rhine). At that time the Allies called it the Ardennes Counteroffensive, and only much later was it called the Battle of the Bulge because of the way the allied front line bulged inward on the wartime news maps. That name stuck, and even to this day the battle, which lasted from December 16, 1944, until January 25, 1945, is referred to as the *Battle of the Bulge*.

I have done some research, and it seems that Kurt started listening to the radio exactly on December 16, when the German counterattack began, which took the Allies completely by surprise. He was able to give us his daily reports at supper. That was so much better than all the rumors and the bragging reports of the Oberkommando der Wehrmacht.

Naturally, Kurt immediately started to search for the BBC, and I ran for my big German bed pillow and threw it over the radio and Kurt's head. But the danger of being overheard by the bugs in our telephone jacks was not great anymore. The much-feared Gestapo had other things to do than to listen to the conversations of a much-needed doctor, which after all had not yielded anything in eight years.

My mother and I had not had any long conversations in our secret little room for well over a year. We knew we could trust our staff, and those few refugees who actually communicated with my mother were always asking whether the Soviets were advancing and had little interest in what was happening in the West.

Nobody was afraid of the western Allies. I cannot stress that enough. By the end of 1944—actually, starting with Pearl Harbor and the defeat in Stalingrad—only the most blinded, fanatical Nazis still believed in a German victory. People knew that the war would be lost, and the urgent question was whether our part of Germany would fall into the hands of the Soviets or the western Allies.

Many evenings, Kurt and I would lie on the floor with our heads pressed close to that precious radio, and Kurt, in his precise manner, would report on the Nazi advance into northern France.

On Christmas Eve, Minna and my mother joined us in the living room. Instead of sitting around a candle-lit tree, we were all sitting in the dark. I remember it as if it were yesterday.

Listening with one ear to the continuing reports from the BBC, Kurt reported that the intent of the westward thrust of the German army was to split the British and American forces and defeat them separately at a later time. According to the broadcasts coming from Hitler's quarters, the defeat of the Soviets would then be an easy matter. We just shook our heads. The urgent reason for the offensive was to thrust forward through Belgium and regain control of the port of Antwerp, which was the only port on the English Channel through which the Allies could get their supplies.

Although we all knew that Hitler was totally unrealistic, he stubbornly refused to listen to his generals, and it was not a good time at our house for a Christmas celebration. We were afraid.

The news did not get any better all through the holiday season. Finally, on New Year's Day came the reports that the Americans had been resupplied, had gathered their forces, and were on the counterattack. Kurt was wearing his shiny and new-looking boots; my mother brought out a bottle of champagne (I never knew where that came from); and the four of us—Minna, Kurt, my mother, and I—toasted in the New Year. We all knew 1945 would be one of the hardest years of our lives, but we hoped it would bring the end of the war and the fall of the horrible Nazi regime.

After tremendous losses on both sides, by January 25 the Battle of the Bulge was officially over. What was left of the German divisions had retreated to the Siegfried line, and the Soviets had restarted their offensive on the eastern front.

Before the German retreat, around January 10, when I got home from my duty in the military hospital Kurt was gone, and my shortwave radio was back in my bed.

My mother explained that the open infection in his knee had healed, and she had advised him that he should try to get to Hanover while it was still in German hands and before the Allies got there. It was easier to walk and hitch rides through your own retreating army rather than be caught in a battle.

Kurt had my mother's walking stick, the one she always used when we went hiking in the Hartz Mountains, and Minna had packed him a bundle with bread, a piece of meat, and a clean pair of socks. By then I had run out of tears, so I just hugged my mother and Minna and hoped that Kurt would be safe.

I did not hear what happened to Kurt for many years. In fact, I pretty much forgot about him until the mid-1960s, when I traveled to western Germany from California to visit my mother. I asked her, "Whatever happened to Minna?"

She reminded me that she was able to get Minna out of Schwerin just before the Soviets arrived and that she paid Minna a small pension until she died sometime in the fifties. Then she told me about Kurt.

The girl Kurt loved did not heard from him for several months and, like the rest of us who had loved ones fighting on the eastern front, she must have assumed that he had either fallen or was missing in action—which on the eastern battlefront was a fate worse than death.

But Kurt survived and made it safely to Hanover and to his girl before the British arrived. That must have been quite a reunion. They were married after he had gone through the formalities of being a British prisoner. After Minna died my mother had lost all contact with him, but there was no reason to believe that, twenty years later, Kurt and his family were not happy and prosperous in Hanover.

The Winter of 1945

After our quiet but hopeful New Year's Day celebration, we faced the beginning of 1945. On January 2, which was a Tuesday, a back-to-business day, the authorities in Schwerin made the official announcement that all schools, cinemas, and dance halls would stay closed until the spring. Of course, anybody involved in community affairs knew that anyway, since we had helped to convert all the schools into military hospitals. The cinemas had gone dark by the middle of December, and nobody had gone dancing in the dance halls for months.

It has never ceased to amaze me how stupid the Nazis thought the German people were. Yes, a large part of the population had been impressed with the social promises and the victories all over Europe, but things had turned for the worse years prior, and there were now only a very few fanatics who still believed in the Nazi miracle.

The rumor mills did the rest. Everybody listened to the rumor mills, and those rumors did not come just from word of mouth, but were constantly fed by those who listened to their shortwave radios and were brave enough to pass the news along. People knew that the rumor mills were by far the best and fastest source of news, and although the information was not always accurate, we were all convinced that we got more of the truth that way than from any of the official communications. The German propaganda was bordering on the ridiculous.

The Allies were closing in on both fronts, heating fuel was unavailable to civilian households, and every night the air-raid sirens howled as the Royal Air Force made its way to Berlin for its relentless bombing of that city. Although at the time no bombs were dropped on Schwerin, the population was hungry, cold, afraid, and extremely weary as they sat in their basements every night until the "all clear" signal sounded.

The closing of the schools freed a lot of teenagers to work for the Vaterland, and boys over sixteen were immediately drafted into the army. We girls were given the option to work in a munitions factory, to serve at the railroad station, or to volunteer for the Red Cross and become a nurse's aide. The latter was by far the best option, but you needed special qualifications to be accepted.

I had worked in my mother's office for years, and I was very lucky to be able to work in a military hospital.

Some of my classmates had no choice and had to work in a munitions factory, and some of them were actually driven in army trucks into the surrounding villages to help the farmers. That was a pathetic joke. The women on the farms whose husbands and sons had been drafted did not need any "help" from city girls who might know Latin and mathematics but had never milked a cow or lifted a pitchfork. To them these girls were just another mouth to feed, and they were simply told to go home. I heard descriptions of those walks home, sometimes over fifty-mile treks without provisions and in the freezing cold.

The hardest and most heartbreaking duty was done by those teenage girls who were assigned to the railroad station. The descriptions of the overcrowded refugee trains were horrendous. The girls were supposed to hand out coffee and sandwiches, but most of the time they had only water to give. One of my girlfriends told me, on one of the rare occasions when we had the chance to get together, that she was working on the platform when a loudly crying woman called out to her. The woman had a bundle in her hands and sobbed, "This is my baby girl, and she died. They won't let me keep her on the train. Will you please take her? My little boy is still on this train, and I can't leave him."

Ingrid was seventeen years old and had never held a baby in her arms, and now she was holding a dead baby. As the refugee train slowly pulled out of the station, she swore that she could hear the mother's crying until the train was out of sight.

I was the only one of our group who got hospital duty, and although it was no piece of cake, it was bearable. After having assisted my mother so much in her office, at least I knew what I was doing. The nurse in charge was an elderly, thoughtful, and experienced woman who wisely assigned me to the officers' ward. In spite of all the Nazi talk, class distinction and a different set of manners was still very much a way of life at that time.

The officers' ward was really just a classroom with twenty cots and a large table in the center. There were only two or three chairs, and at mealtime the men would sit at the end of their cots and maneuver the table and the cots so that they could all sit around the table and eat their meager meals from tin plates. If they wanted water with their meal, they had to share the two glasses we had. I brought the water from a tap out in the hall and refilled the glasses when they were empty. To this day, Germans are not enthusiastic water drinkers, and I know all of them would have greatly preferred beer, but as I look back on it now, we were probably pretty lucky to have drinkable water at all.

Part of the job of a nurse's aide was to sweep the floor and wash the coffee cups. Well, they watched me handle a broom for the first time—and it was indeed for the first time in my life—and one of the ambulatory officers, who was at least a major, took the broom away from me and did the job himself. I never had to handle the darned thing again, and it was the same with those coffee cups.

But they all recognized the fact that I was very, very good when it came to tending to wounds, and I never once flinched at all the pus, the maggots, and the smell. And I sat with their dying comrades, holding their hands and kissing their foreheads when they were crying out for their mothers before they drew their last breath. They all sat and watched me when I did that; they respected me and did not give a hoot that I was a totally inadequate housekeeper.

I was now part of the military, but as a local I did not have to sleep in the nurses' room where the bunks were stacked four high and the bedding never changed. I could go home at night, hug my mother and Minna, get a decent meal, and sleep in my own bed. And of course, continue my nightly telephone duty and listen to my shortwave radio.

The broadcasts from my German officer at the BBC were becoming fewer and fewer as the British army penetrated deeper into Germany, but we did hear about the dreadful firebombing of Dresden in February, which was so much worse than the firebombing of Hamburg.

We also heard about the conference at Yalta in February. There, a sick President Roosevelt; Winston Churchill, the British prime minister, who knew that he was on the way out; and a triumphant Stalin, whose forces were only about forty miles from Berlin, had made decisions about the fate of the defeated Germany— decisions that would haunt Germany and the Allies for decades to come.

I don't remember much about March. I went to work, listened to the cries of the wounded and the cries of those who had lost yet another loved one, and pulled the feather bed over my head at night, knowing that for better or worse, the end was in sight.

The Bombing of Schwerin

Our lives went on as normally as possible. Our little town did not have to endure the horrors of the day-and-night bombing of the industrial centers of Germany. There was nothing to bomb. No factories, no railroad centers, no troop transports. All we had were fields, lakes, and small houses.

Starting in January 1945, the endless trains brought not only refugees and displaced persons but also hundreds of wounded and dying soldiers from the eastern front. Thanks to our out-of-the-way location, even the horror trains destined for the concentration camps passed us by.

The air-raid sirens sounded pretty much every night when the British bombers made their way to Berlin, but it was only when we heard a lot of shooting that we would go into the basement. We had some flak (antiaircraft guns), and once, early in the war, I saw a plane shot down, but on the whole our people knew that if we did not bother the bombers, they would not bother us.

Much later in my life I learned that this attitude, which was not terribly patriotic and not at all in accordance with Nazi doctrine, probably saved our little town. When I went to the university in

England I met a young Royal Air Force pilot. His wartime experiences, constantly bombing the German civilian population, had made him somewhat what we used to call shell-shocked. Now we would say that he was suffering from post-traumatic stress disorder.

When he finally got around to asking me where I had been during the war and I answered, "Schwerin, northwest of Berlin," he said, to my astonishment, "Schwerin? I know Schwerin!"

He then told me that when the RAF flew during the night to attack Berlin, they had to take the shortest route to get there, along the River Elbe. But when they returned, they took the slightly longer, but much safer, northern route via Schwerin, where they did not have to worry about flak. And if they had any bombs left over, they were instructed not to drop them on Schwerin. The little town, surrounded by lakes, was a good guide and on a moonlit night looked beautiful with its castle sitting on an island. Well, you could have knocked me down with a feather, and I thanked him for sparing my town.

Unfortunately for us, the Americans did not have the same sentiments, as they were trying to outrace the Soviets and occupy as much of Germany as possible.

On April 17, a bright and sunny day, they launched their only attack on Schwerin. It was a totally unexpected nightmare.

The warning sirens sounded too late, the few antiaircraft guns we had were not manned during the day, and the people could not make it to their basements before the bombs started to fall.

The raid lasted no more than twenty minutes, but in that short time 217 civilians were killed and forty houses were totally destroyed. The tram and bus depot was severely damaged, which meant that there was no public transportation for several weeks to come. And, as the American bombers departed, the remaining bombs were dropped on the cemetery.

I went to the bombed area the next day and saw all the bodies laid out in shrouds at the entrance of the cemetery, ready for burial. Teenagers were working, and they first had to rebury all the skulls and bones that were lying about before they could start to dig the graves for the air-raid victims. The graves of my grandfather and my two uncles, who had fallen in the First World War, were gutted, and I found the pieces of their broken tombstones scattered about. I did not know how to tell my grandmother about this. It all happened when the town was supposed to be under the protection of the International Red Cross, with a huge Red Cross symbol painted on the roof of every major building.

The British continued their nightly attacks on Berlin, but instead of just rolling over and going back to sleep, we now went to bed fully dressed and made our way to the nearest air-raid shelter when the planes flew over Schwerin. It was quite a long walk for my mother and me, and often when we got there all the benches were taken. For me it always meant sitting on the concrete floor, but my mother was so loved and respected that someone would always offer her his seat. We were all tired and weary, and usually there was deadly silence in the shelter. No one brought a radio, even if they had one, because the radio waves could not penetrate the thick concrete walls, and you never knew if there was a Nazi spy in the crowd. Even complaining about the sleepless nights or the lack of news from the fronts or the shortage of food could have brought on severe punishment. Often, the only sound you heard was the crying of children or the very loud public announcement that the "all clear" had sounded.

The night of April 13, only a few nights after the bombing of Schwerin and one of our first nights in the shelter, the silence was shattered by a sudden burst of the loudspeaker, and we heard that there would be an announcement by the Oberkommando der Wehrmacht.

"The president of the United States, Franklin Delano Roosevelt, died yesterday on April 12."

To our horror, a loud cheer went up, reverberating throughout the air-raid shelter. My mother put her arm around me and whispered, "There goes our last hope."

The last night we spent in the shelter was April 30 when, once more, the loudspeakers penetrated the dreary silence to announce, "Adolf Hitler, the Führer of the German people, died today, April 30, in Berlin." There was not a word about it having been a suicide and that he had been hiding for days in his bullet-and-bomb-safe bunker; just that he had died.

Strangely enough, that announcement was greeted with deadly silence. There were no sounds of sorrow.

We all understood that the world as we knew it was crumbling around us and would never be the same again. Not because Hitler had committed suicide, but because Germany was losing the war—a war that it should not have started in the first place.

The Saddest Story I Ever Heard

Early in April 1945 there was a knock at our front door, which also was the door to my mother's medical office. Since it was late afternoon and the staff had gone off duty, I opened the door.

Six people were standing there—one young man and five women of indeterminable age—and they indicated by their gestures that they would like to come into the house. They looked like refugees. Since it was the end of the war, refugees from East Prussia and other eastern countries were everywhere. These people were fleeing before the advancing Russian army, and their request to be let in did not surprise me. They didn't appear to be German, and they were completely silent. They looked rugged and desperate and, of course, I brought them into the house and seated them in my mother's waiting room.

After they were seated, and after we had looked at each other for a little while, the young man started to speak in educated German and told me, "We were turned loose from the concentration camp, and we have run and walked for several days and nights. We could hear the guns of the fighting armies."

I found out that they were Polish. The young man had been a

medical student who had demonstrated against the Nazi occupation, while the women had done nothing. Their only offense was the fact that they were probably Jewish. They never said anything and just sat there with their huge sad eyes, shivering and crying silently.

Fortunately, my mother returned from her house calls and immediately took charge. She told Minna to make a big pot of potato soup with all the sausage we had in the house, and she told me to help the women take a bath. We had only one bathtub in the house, and hot water was in short supply, so I bathed them two at a time. Seeing those pathetic, emaciated, and shivering bodies was one of the most upsetting experiences of my eighteen-year-old life and now, more than seventy years later, I have not forgotten a single moment of it.

That night, the young man, whose name I never knew, asked me, "Now do you want to know?"

We sat on the stairs until deep into the night, and I heard for the first time what really went on in the concentration camps. The young man needed to talk, and I was glad that I was there and able to listen.

The people arrived in trains, one thousand souls at a time. They were herded off the train, told to strip off their clothing and hand over all their possessions, and were taken to the showers naked. Then there were the screams, and then the smoke and the stench.

The young man had to sort the clothes—one box for women, one box for men, one for children, and one for babies. One box was for toys, one for jewelry, one for false teeth, and one for "other possessions."

There was one train per hour and ten trains a day; every one transported exactly one thousand human beings—men, women, and children, old and young. This went on for weeks, until the Russians came and the gates were opened and people were told to run.

He did not spare me a single gruesome detail of what had gone on in that camp of horrors. I listened almost the entire night, motionless, because I had long since lost the ability to cry. Nothing published in the newspapers, nothing written in books, nothing shown in newsreels, on television, or in films from that day to this has ever surprised or saddened me more, or exceeded what I heard on that unforgettable night.

The next day, when I got back from my duties at the military hospital, our visitors were gone. The young man had said to my mother, "We must go right now because, you see, we are even more afraid of the Russian soldiers than we are of the Germans."

That evening I went to my mother's room and told her what I had heard. While I was unable to cry, she finally cried bitterly and said that she had always known that horrible things were going on, but none of us knew just exactly how unspeakable it really was. I am one of those people who believe in a national guilt and responsibility; even though I didn't participate, I shall carry that burden of guilt to the end of my life.

The Amis Are Coming!

Only the people in western Mecklenburg could say that they had three different armies of occupation in three months at the end of World War II. Those of us living in Schwerin, the capital of Mecklenburg, had that experience, and even now, after over seventy years, it is interesting to reflect on the intrinsic difference and style of the Americans, the British, and the Soviets as occupying forces.

At the conference of Yalta, in February 1945, it was decided that Germany would be divided into four zones. The British would be in the northwest, the Americans in the west and southwest, the Soviets in the east, and France—whose Vichy government was questionable—would get a narrow section along the French border, which was carved out of the British and American Zones. The American troops either failed (or didn't want) to get the message that defined the border of the territory they were supposed to occupy, and they moved much too far ahead, deep into Mecklenburg, the Harz Mountains, and Thuringia.

When I left the house early in the morning of May 2, the streets were empty and eerily quiet. The refugees were either in the houses or had left town in fear of the approaching Soviet army.

As I stood still to take in the strange and unusual scene, I could hear a faint rumbling sound on my left; it sounded like distant thunder, and I realized that it came from the east and therefore must be the Soviet front. Then my face must have lit up, because on my right, from the west—the American side—I could hear a rumbling sound too.

I stood perfectly still and concentrated on listening, hoping to hear whether the sound coming from the west was perhaps just a tiny bit louder, meaning that the Americans would be closer than the feared Soviets. The rumbling from the west seemed to get fainter, then there did not seem to be any sound from that direction at all.

I realized that my fear was making my mind play games and that I was hearing things that were not even there. Then I started to run and run—I could run very fast with all that ballet training—and arrived totally breathless in my officers' ward at the hospital. They all gathered around me and kept asking, "Did you see any Russians? Are there tanks? Have you heard if they are going to surrender this town, or will there be a battle?"

One officer, the one who had taken the broom from me and still did the sweeping up, put his arm around my shoulder and said, "Let her catch her breath. She will tell us what she knows when she can, and in the meantime we are going to sit here and wait, just as we have done for the past forty-eight hours." And that is exactly what we did.

The chief of staff and the head nurse went from room to room and told us to stay inside and await further instructions. It was as deadly quiet in that hospital as it had been outside.

We waited for many hours, and then the most incredible thing happened. A strange and unknown smell drifted into our room, and one of my officers, who had been to America, shouted, "That's Virginian tobacco; I'd know that anywhere. The *Amis* are here!"

The German soldier who was smoking that miracle told us how he had just left the hospital and gone outside to see what was going on. Every officer in our room, from the second lieutenant to the colonel, rolled their eyes or covered their smile, and the corporal went on, undisturbed.

". . . and then I saw this American soldier, and he saw me. He looked at my arm in the sling, took out a cigarette, and lit it for me. That's all."

I covered my face with my hands, another nurse's aide came running in and we hugged each other and said, *"Das Schlimmste ist vorbei."* (The worst is over.) That was not exactly true, but the Americans were there now, and we never had the slightest doubt that we would be safe for the time being.

In another part of town, just after noon, a very different scene had taken place, and I can tell it word for word because the daughter of the commanding officer of Schwerin was and is my best girlfriend (Gerda, whom I mentioned earlier), and I have heard the story many times, both from her and from her father. I am telling the story exactly as it was told to me.

Major Keller got the report that the American forces were north of Ludwigslust, about eighteen miles south of Schwerin, and were approaching the town in jeeps and without tanks or visible heavy weapons. The American ground forces appeared to have been informed that Schwerin was a hospital city and that it would be in compliance with the Red Cross instructions, there would be no weapons, and the city would not be defended.

Just to make absolutely sure, Major Keller instructed his aide, Lieutenant Neumann, to bring a white flag, and they drove to the edge of the town to await the Americans. In short order, two jeeps showed up. A young lieutenant jumped out of one, saluted casually, and indicated to the Germans to put the white flag away.

He said, "Your city is mine, whether I shoot or not. We will talk about that later, but first give me those kid gloves, your watch, and your ring."

Their eyes were locked as the immaculately dressed German major, the commandant of the city of Schwerin, pulled off his gloves finger by finger, unfastened his gold watch, and took off the cherished family signet ring, which his young daughter put on his little finger before he left for the front. He handed them to the young, relaxed American lieutenant in battle fatigues who spoke surprisingly good German.

Major Keller said, "I came to surrender our town Schwerin in order to avoid bloodshed and destruction. The town is practically undamaged, and every school has been converted into a military hospital to receive our wounded from the Soviet front.

Do I have your word?"

"You have my word. I have no intention of fighting. You see, I have just a few men and our jeeps. No heavy ammunition and no tanks. However, I am sorry to say that I am going to have to take you prisoner. We will establish a temporary POW camp over on the tennis court."

The major smiled. The tennis court was at the club where he and his wife had spent many hours playing tennis and usually had a drink in the clubhouse afterwards. "My house is close by. Will you permit me to go home and pick up my shaving kit, my pajamas, and a change of clothes?"

"Of course. Two of my men will go with you."

Two GIs were called and walked with the major to his nearby villa. The major was secretly grateful that he had taken a fellow officer's advice to drive his wife and beautiful seventeen-year-old daughter, as well as several other officers' wives and children, westward to the safe haven that he knew would become the British Zone of Germany.

The major picked up what he needed and put it in a small suitcase while the GIs, who were curious and visibly impressed, followed him into every room. Quite possibly, Major Keller became the only prisoner of war who was able to start his imprisonment with his shaving kit and pajamas.

We now had American occupation, but the Nazi terror was not over yet.

As I walked home that evening and crossed the square in front of the railroad station, I saw a body hanging from a lamppost. People were rushing by, averting their eyes. Later, I found out that it was the body of a schoolteacher, a refugee by the name of Marianne Grunthal. She was hanged one hour before the American arrival because she had said after Hitler's death, "Thank God, now we shall have peace."

Germany surrendered to the western Allies on May 7 and to the Soviets on May 9.

For my country, the war was over.

The GI from Ohio

From May 2 until June 1 we were under American occupation. We called them the Amis, and since we had no personal dealings with anybody above the rank of corporal, we soon thought of them as our happy and sometimes naughty boys.

As soon as they arrived in town they got out of their jeeps, mixed with the people, and asked everyone they met on the street if they had a Leica or any other kind of camera. They took everybody's wristwatch and pointed to any golden rings a woman might be wearing. They actually made those women, whose husbands and fiancés were at the front, take off their wedding bands, and they took them away from them. That was cruel, but by that time all of us knew what the German soldiers had done in Russia and Poland, and this was nothing by comparison.

We hoped and prayed that there would be no violence.

Within a couple of days people learned to keep their watches at home, and the women who did not want to be parted from their wedding bands hid them in the top of their stockings. There was never any violence as long as you showed your empty hands before you were even asked and smiled. The Ami would shrug his shoulders and let you go on your way.

I have often been asked whether there was any rape, and my answer has always been, "No need! The Amis had chewing gum." So much for German womanhood, but these were the times of war. Under Hitler, chewing gum had been forbidden, and propaganda pointed out that chewing gum was just one more bit of American decadence. It did not matter whether you were a Nazi or an extreme nationalist or not—in spite of all the propaganda, we all loved chewing gum. You did not have to jump into bed with an Ami to get a stick of gum. I found that a friendly smile went a long way.

The American commanding officer moved into the offices of the German commanding officer downtown, and together they kept the water running, the electric power going, and some sort of order on the crowded streets. For all of us, the awful fear of the approaching Soviet army left for the time being. Schweriners now showed up on the street unafraid of air raids and anxious to meet those interesting Americans, who were all over town and appeared to be just as anxious to meet the Germans.

We must not forget that over the previous century many Germans had immigrated to America, and a large percentage of the occupying Americans had at least one German grandparent. The Amis spoke or understood a little German, and most educated Germans, especially the younger ones, spoke some English.

Hitler and his cohorts had been planning to rule the world. They knew very well that this could not be achieved using the

German language, and therefore English was taught intensively at all middle and high schools right to the end of the war. Verbal communication between the Amis and the Germans was never a problem. When you look at it that way, you will understand that fraternization was neither difficult nor surprising.

The eighteen thousand concentration camp victims from Sachsenhausen-Oranienburg, who had hidden in the forests around Schwerin hoping for the arrival of the American army, swarmed into our little town. As we all knew, they had been mistreated and abused by their German captors, and they did not trust any of us. Only a few, like my mother and I, knew how horrendous it had been.

They all needed food and shelter, and a large number needed medical care, and that is where my mother worked her wonders. Everybody who left our house had a little bit of their trust and dignity restored. They all wanted to leave Schwerin and go to where they were sure no Russians could reach them, and my mother used her connections. With the help of the Americans, and later the British, almost all of the concentration camp victims were gone and safely in the West within less than two months.

Most of our household help had returned home to their villages, and Minna did a yeoman's job in the kitchen mostly on her own. My mother had two faithful helpers in the office who went back to their families in town as soon as I got home from my job in the evening and could take over.

There was not much time for contemplation, and that was just as well.

Most of my memories of that time are a blur, but there was one incident that stands out clearly, maybe because it moved me. I have told it so often that it comes to mind when I think of the Amis.

We were about one week into the American occupation, and I had just returned home from work and was trying to get cleaned up when one of the patients knocked on the bedroom door and said, "Tante Doctor would like you to come downstairs."

As I entered my mother's office and examining room, I saw an American soldier sitting on her gynecological examination chair, his legs dangling. He was drumming some sort of rhythm on the chrome stirrups, which were permanently in the up position on the 1930s version of that particular contraption.

My mother had called me in to help with the translation. She correctly assumed that my high school English would be better than what she remembered of hers. She also knew that I had seen so much in the last year that nothing would shock my eighteen-year-old ears. The following conversation ensued.

"Why are you here?" I asked him.

"A woman sent me." He gave her name, which my mother duly noted. "I think I got her in trouble."

I did a double take on that one. The Amis had been in town for only five days. How fast did these guys work? Could he be thinking that he already got her pregnant?

It was a delicate subject, and I was afraid that my high school

English was not up to the task. My mother raised her eyebrows and told me, almost whispering, "This woman has two children and a husband on the Russian front. She is probably very afraid that her husband might return and find her pregnant."

I asked him, "What do you want us to do?"

"Give her something."

I was grateful that he did not appear to be a man of many words, since I had a hard time understanding him. "There is nothing I can do now," I translated for my mother, "but I will keep my eye on her. Maybe we can arrange something later at the military hospital." This time he had a hard time understanding me, but I thought that I finally got it across to him.

The soldier kept sitting on the gyno-chair and seemed to want to carry on the conversation, so I asked him, "Where are you from?"

That was the easiest part of the conversation, because it was practically the first English sentence I had learned. The answer was harder to deal with, and he had to say it three times before I got it.

"Ohio."

I had never even heard of Ohio, and his Ohio dialect and my high school German-Oxford accent were miles apart. I learned only recently that the people in Ohio pronounce it "Ohia." No wonder! I would not get that even now.

"Are you a nurse?" he asked. "You are wearing the Red Cross on your cap."

"Yes, I help at the Beethoven-School Military Hospital."

"What time do you go to work?"

I wondered why he asked, but I answered, "I leave at six o'clock in the morning and get home at about eight in the evening." I could see that my mother was uncomfortable that I had given out that information, but he was *Occupation,* and we made a real effort to be helpful and friendly without getting ourselves into trouble.

"That's not safe for a young girl. I'll be here at six." With that, our Ami soldier slid off the gyno-chair, looked into every cupboard, obviously intrigued by the medical instruments, and said, "See you," and was out the door.

The next morning I had almost forgotten what he had said, but there he was at our front door. He raised his hand and escorted me wordlessly to the military hospital. He ignored all the hoots and whistles from his fellow GIs, who obviously thought that he had made some sort of a catch at 6:00 a.m.

Apart from asking me, "What time?" he never spoke another word to me, but he was there every morning and every night, and when he could not come himself another wordless GI would materialize and be my silent escort. That lasted for the remaining three weeks of the American occupation.

When the Amis had to leave, I missed that almost childlike tact and gentleness, which was so different from the horrors of war I had seen. I hope that the gentle man from Ohio never lost his decent, caring nature and that he got home safely.

British Occupation

From what I heard many years later, there were some serious discussions between the British and the American commands, and the Americans were in trouble because of their unauthorized push deep into Mecklenburg, the Harz Mountains, and Thuringia. The German people loved it and were intensely grateful, but in view of the Yalta Conference, strategically this was an untenable situation.

On June 1 our Amis were replaced by the British—the *Tommies* as we called them. The change of command happened so quietly overnight that at first we did not even know the difference. But there was a difference, and it became quite evident in a very short time.

The British had been colonizing for centuries; they had years and years of history and training, and they knew what to do. Their approach was quite different from that of the Americans. There was no more fraternizing. No more, "Hello, Fraulein," first thing in the morning, no more hoots and whistles, no tongue clicking. Every Tommy looked straight ahead—in fact, looked right through you and went on his efficient way.

At the time we thought that the behavior of the British was really strange, especially since we had got along so well with the Americans. We did not know until much later that General Eisenhower, the commander of all the forces in Europe, had issued strict antifraternization orders.

At first no member of the armed forces was allowed to speak to any German or Austrian civilian. In June they were allowed to speak to children, and in July they were allowed to speak to adults, but only strictly on business. In August the ban was lifted in both Germany and Austria. It is funny to know that the British followed the orders of the American general in every detail, while the American troops just ignored them.

On the second day of British occupation we had our first roll call at the hospital. All medical and nursing personnel had to line up by rank. I did not even know that I had such a thing as a rank and went to the end of the line. I always went to the end of the line because that was my place anyway. I was always the shortest person wherever I was. We were called by name, and all of us were officially declared British prisoners of war.

On the third day street cars and buses were running, and on the fourth day all concentration camp survivors had identity cards, which entitled them to be first in line at the endless queues in front of the grocer, the butcher, and the baker.

This caused some considerable grumbling amongst the locals and the few refugees who were still in town. The British took no nonsense, and two or three Tommies watched those lines, standing rigid and expressionless, and as far as I know nothing got out of hand.

We were never officially told, but my mother knew that it would only be a matter of time when the British would have to leave and the Soviets would take over. She helped as many people as she could to get out of town to the West.

Minna left by refugee train to be with her brother in Osnabrück. We knew for sure that Hanover and Osnabrück—in fact, all of Westphalia—would be in the British Zone. My mother asked me if I wanted to go with Minna. She said that at this point she could easily arrange it, but I sternly refused. I promised my mother and myself that as long as she stayed in Schwerin I would stay too.

I did not understand why my mother had tears in her eyes when she hugged me and said, *"Wir wissen das nicht. Vielleicht steht etwas anderes in den Sternen geschrieben."* (We don't know. Maybe something else is written in the stars.)

The Horror Is Here

On July 1 we heard distant shooting, and on July 2 we watched with horror from our front window as the British commandant, immaculate and erect, handed our city over to a Russian officer. They both saluted, and the British marched out in step while the Soviets dragged in.

They were a sorrowful lot, and if we had not been so afraid of them I could have pitied them. There were, as far as I could see, no motorized vehicles except for one tank, and the few major weapons they had were pushed by soldiers who looked to us as if they had been recruited directly from Outer Mongolia.

There was a regiment of women wearing no shoes, and their feet were wrapped in rags. They were not at all like the Russian women soldiers, whose reputation for fierceness and cruelty preceded them. Many a German soldier had told me that they were not afraid to fight the Russian men, but oh my god, the women!

I stayed at home with my mother that day, and together we cringed at the pounding at the door and watched the Mongolian types swarming all over our house, ripping out the telephones, stealing the radio and the typewriter, and helping themselves to all the food they could find.

For years I wondered what they did with all those telephones and typewriters, which did not even have the Cyrillic alphabet, but I understand that big trainloads of loot went to the Soviet Union and probably disappeared on the black market.

That night I did something I had not done for years. I crawled into bed with my mother, and for the last time in my life I was her baby and we both took comfort in that feeling. We knew that tomorrow would be another day and that it would not be any easier than today, but at least we were together.

We woke up to a terrific racket in front of our house, and as we looked out the window we saw one of the Mongolian types inside my mother's car, trying to get it started; some others were howling encouragement and dancing around our little car.

My mother said, "I'd better get down there and take care of this."

She got dressed, got her car keys, and went out the front door, and as I watched from the window she handed the man her keys and said in an icy voice, "Would you like me to start it for you?"

All of a sudden there was deadly silence. The howling types slinked away, and the man in the car shook his head, took the keys, and started the car. Our beloved little DKW stuttered down the road, and we could still hear it after it had gone out of sight.

For six years of war and two months of American and British occupation, that little car had been safe in front of our house. It had done its duty for so many patients and refugees, and it took the Russians only twenty-four hours to steal and destroy it. My mother found the car only hours later not far from our house, driven into a wall and totally wrecked.

When I tried to hug and comfort her she looked me straight in the eyes and said seriously, "We brought this on ourselves. The German people deserve what they are getting. There are consequences." She kept that thought for the rest of her life, and I had to learn to live with it.

I left the house at my usual time, somehow feeling secure in my nurses' uniform, and without looking right or left I walked the two miles to the hospital and came home just before dark.

I don't know how I did it, but I was numb, and like a machine I did that for three more days until the Soviets closed the hospital.

To my astonishment, after the Russian occupation was only two days old I saw more and more young German men wearing red ties, a red handkerchief in their shirt pocket, or a small red ribbon on their caps. When I asked my mother about that, she explained that it was a code to let everyone know that they were Communist sympathizers. She said that it had been exactly the same before Hitler came to power, and that these men were not Communists at all. After all, she had worked in the Resistance long enough to know every secret Communist in town. They were just trying to gain some political advantage. I encountered the same thing in the British Zone a little later where young men, who had answered to Hans or Heinz quite happily all their life, now wanted to be called Harry.

I was disgusted but never mentioned it except to my mother. Those times under the Soviets were just as dangerous as the Hitler years.

At the hospital all of my patients, as well as the personnel, felt this threat, and you heard the cry, "We have got to get out of here!" They cried it out over and over, and it got worse when the horror stories started to make their rounds. In a nearby town the Russians had shot the severely wounded soldiers in their beds and locked the nurses in a room and raped them for hours. We could hear artillery fire in the distance, and we saw smoke literally all around our town. We were like caged animals, but nobody could see any way of escape.

After a few days of not so quiet desperation, we could see why we had been spared. Schwerin was undestroyed and intact, and the Russians started to move their wounded into our hospitals and their troops into our military barracks. All of the German wounded were herded into one big dance hall quite near to our house, and we went to work under the most deplorable conditions. There were some bunks four beds high, but most of the wounded had to lie on the floor; if they were lucky, they had some straw to lie on. After a while we had to remove the straw bit by bit because the bare floors were easier to clean than the filthy straw.

I did not dare ask where the nurses slept, because I guessed how they must have felt, knowing that the chief medical officer and I were the only lucky ones who lived in Schwerin. Although we were both prisoners of war, we had permission to go home at night.

Conditions in that converted dance hall were dreadful, and the toilet facilities were pitiful. The dance hall, as with so many venues in northern Germany, had been ill equipped with only two or three stalls. I was always so grateful to the German soldiers who pulled cleaning duty because, wounded as they were, they kept those few toilets amazingly clean for us women. It was an act of chivalry in all that mess. The hundreds of wounded men went in the backyard or out into the street at night.

We completely ran out of bandages and used toilet paper instead to cover the wounds until we ran out of that too. My mother went around to her patients and all the neighbors and asked every household to tear up one bedsheet for bandages. There were no more Nazi and anti-Nazi households. We were all in this together. I took those bandages home and boiled and washed them at night, but with the number of wounded it was like a drop in the bucket.

Once in a while we would receive a shipment of bread, and we nurses had the responsibility of spreading some weird sausage stuff on the bread while the men watched our every move, as if we would have dared to pop even the tiniest piece of bread into our mouths. Food was in desperately short supply, and they were all starving. Some of our men went out at night and caught cats and dogs. I knew that they skinned them in the backyard right behind the dance hall and cooked them in a huge caldron with some dehydrated cabbage. I stayed away from that back door as best I could.

I did have to eat that stew once when I could not make it home because of fighting in the street. Now I can say that, along with horseflesh, I have eaten cats and dogs too, but I do not talk about that very often.

Every night as I walked home—and I mean walked, since I did not dare to draw attention to myself by running—I was scared to death of what might await me around the next corner. I hypnotized myself with a little prayer, which I said over and over, *"Danke Gott dass ich nach Hause gehen kann."* (Thank you, God, that I can go home.) Amazingly, that helped. I was always grateful to get home at night, and the memory of warmth and love I felt there has been with me through all my often turbulent and upsetting life.

After my mother greeted me, she immediately took me into our bedroom to delouse me. Fortunately, I never had head lice—my nurse's cap protected me from those—but it was impossible not to be infected by body lice. The filthy straw, the unwashed clothes, the total absence of showers, the casts that were never changed, and the open wounds with their pus and fluids did their job of breeding lice and maggots. I was incredibly lucky to be able to go home at night, to get one good meal, and to have a mother who lovingly picked the body lice off of me and out of my underwear every night.

As far as the outside world was concerned, we knew absolutely nothing. My shortwave radio was gone, along with all other means of communication. There were no blaring loudspeakers and, naturally, no newspapers. The rumor mills never stopped, and it seemed to me that all the news was bad and scary.

One day in early August a German soldier asked a question that made me stop in my tracks, and I asked him to repeat it. He said, "I asked, 'So, when is he coming back?'"

"Who is supposed to come back?"

"The Tommy, of course; he promised."

I sat down with the soldier and asked him to tell me the whole story. It seems that he had been in the room when a British officer said goodbye to the doctor in charge, declaring, "We will be back, I promise." The conversation had been very low-key and in English, and nobody had paid any attention to the private who was a high school student and knew some English.

"What do you suppose he meant?" I asked.

"I don't know, he just promised that they would be back, and it has been a whole month!"

Naturally, I told my mother about that, and she said that she had heard similar things but had not said anything because she did not dare to believe in good rumors.

So we just waited and hoped that for once a good rumor could be true.

Leaving Home

We waited and we waited.

We heard from our Soviet captors that the Americans had dropped an atomic bomb on Hiroshima on August 6 and a second one on Nagasaki on August 9. We did not really know what that meant, and neither did the Russians, but we were told that it caused a great deal of tension between the western Allies and the Soviets, and the rumors started that there might be a war between East and West.

I now spent the nights at the hospital, because the Russian hostility against the Germans, who so openly sided with the western Allies, had become so intense that we did not dare leave our *Gefängnis* (prison), as we called it.

One evening my mother appeared and spoke briefly to our physician in charge. He called me into his office and left us alone. My mother handed me a small suitcase, took my face into both her hands, and said, "My only darling child, I won't see you for a very long time. This suitcase contains a first aid kit, and since you are in a nurse's uniform it should pass inspection. Take good care of it and do not open it until you are safely in the

British Zone and alone in a room.

I have talked to Doctor Gerlach, and he will see to it that your name is on the list of German prisoners to be transported to the British Zone. Officially you should stay here because you are registered in Schwerin and have a home. They have too many refugees and POWs in the British Zone already. Get in touch with your father in England through the International Red Cross in Switzerland. Your father will take care of you."

I did not fully understand at the time that my mother had gotten the word that the British were coming to Schwerin to bring their prisoners to the British Zone.

I hugged my mother, not realizing that it was for the last time for many years, but I did sense how incredibly difficult this was for her. My parents' breakup thirteen years prior had been complete, and I had not heard my father's name mentioned by my mother during all that time. She handed me a note in her barely legible doctor's writing. It said:

Dr. med. Otto Marienfeld, Papworth Hall, England
Familie Schnoor bombed out and returned to Hamburg
Tula Heinemann refugee from Schwerin, in
Hamburg-Blankenese

The next morning there was a cry that went from mouth to mouth in the crowded ballroom; "The British Red Cross train is leaving from the *Bahnhof* in one hour at 13:30 sharp!"

We left the military hospital, our temporary prison, on foot. There were approximately 250 wounded soldiers. The nursing personnel and some twenty or thirty ambulatory POWs helped to carry some of the stretchers. We were all struggling to keep up with the fast-paced British soldiers who were leading and guarding us on the one-mile walk to the station. We had to dodge Russian vehicles and soldiers and the so very many refugees who arrived daily.

I was out of breath, my heart was pounding, and there were tears in my eyes as I squeezed myself into a narrow seat between two wounded soldiers. I was grateful that I made it to the train and that I was able to get on board with all the pushing and shoving and noise. My folded coat was behind my back, my mother's tiny suitcase was on my lap, and my feet were resting on a duffle bag. Two soldiers had carried the bag on board and placed it ever so carefully in the aisle between the seats. Just as the train was about to glide out of the station, one soldier whispered in my ear, "Be careful, my girlfriend is in that bag."

I never did see my mother, who I am sure was standing on the platform until the train pulled out of the station, hoping for one last look at her only child. Now I was sitting in the crowded compartment of the Red Cross prisoner transport train sent by the British army.

Here I was, eighteen years old and dressed in a nurse's uniform. It was a gray and white striped dress, a white bib apron held in place by two large safety pins, and a gray cap, which covered all my hair and had a big Red Cross in front. My overcoat and that small suitcase were my only possessions as I left my home and everything I had ever known and understood. It was a good thing that I did not know at that moment that it would be over forty years before I could return.

I closed my eyes so that I would not have to see St. Paul's church, the Ostorfer Lake, and the bicycle path I had taken so many times as they slid by. Oh, so many memories!

The important thing now was to relax and hope that my papers were in order for the British MPs. They were coming through the train, patiently climbing over luggage and wounded soldiers, and I held my breath, hoping that they would not find the girl who was hiding stock-still in a duffle bag at my feet.

Suddenly, there was gunfire.

We all dove to the floor, and I tried to throw myself on top of the girl in the duffle bag to shield her. I could hardly breathe, there was so much weight on top of me, and I wondered about her.

The Americans had dropped their atom bombs on Hiroshima and Nagasaki, apparently forgetting to notify the Soviets be-forehand, and the Soviets had intentionally forgotten about the armistice with Germany and that the British and Americans were once their allies.

The Soviets attacked our train with gunfire at every railroad crossing and at every little village it passed. Above, we could hear the buzzing of one lonely airplane. Our train was clearly marked as a Red Cross train, but the Soviet occupation forces had assured us often enough that the Red Cross meant nothing to them. So now we were wondering whether the Soviets would add some bombs to their attack. But nothing happened. Maybe the plane was just on a reconnaissance mission.

In spite of all the shooting, no one was injured, and I did not even see any broken windows. I did not think much about it then, but later I wondered if these attacks had been only scare tactics and general harassment with the Soviets deliberately missing the train. I shall never know.

When the gunfire stopped, the MPs calmly continued their inspection. Miraculously, everyone's papers were in order, and the train pulled slowly over the invisible borderline that would divide East Germany (the German Democratic Republic) from West Germany (the Federal Republic of Germany) for forty-four years. Germany divided, the industrial area separated from its breadbasket!

Now that we were across the border, the soldier with the duffle bag pushed all our feet out of the way and tenderly opened the zipper. The girl inside was fighting for breath. She looked frightened and disheveled; her face was wet with tears. Still, the soldier took her in his arms and kissed her and kissed her.

"Give her a chance to breathe first," I wanted to say, but then, what did I know.

Past the waving fields of rye I could see the steeple of the church of Ratzeburg, and just as I was thinking that Hamburg, our destination, could only be two hours away, even at this crawling pace, the train slowed to a halt, and a voice called, *"Alle aussteigen!"* (Everybody out!)

Nobody questioned the order, and we took our belongings and disembarked.

"Wir werden im Bunker übernachten" (We shall spend the night in the air-raid shelter.), called the same voice.

Okay. I saw an uninviting concrete block with a door across the road from the railroad station, and with soldiers on crutches, arms in slings, and blood-soaked head bandages, we made our way to that one little opening. I was not as swift as usual, and by the time I reached the bowels of that air-raid shelter, all the wooden benches were taken. I slid into a spot against the wall on the concrete floor.

Everybody was building a nest out of whatever items they were able to bring on the trip. Some people actually had a blanket, and some had soft bags that could serve as a pillow, and some soldiers even had backpacks with all sorts of stuff. I never saw that special duffle bag again, and I hoped that the girl and her soldier were safe.

I watched everyone around me and realized that I, too, had to build my little nest and claim my space. Funny how we humans do that, even under the weirdest of circumstances. I folded my coat into a pillow, sat down on it, put my little suitcase at my feet, and took stock of the situation.

It was getting very crowded, so it would not get too cold, and I was glad to see some air vents near the ceiling.

There was a door marked "Toilette" with a *Geschlossen* (closed) sign on it. One soldier tried it anyway, but the door was locked. Nothing doing there. So I did what everyone else was doing. I waited until I could see by the air vents that it was dark outside, picked up my coat and my suitcase, and found a bush outside. The area around the railroad station would be a disgusting place in the morning, and the locals would be swearing at the uncivilized refugees *aus dem Osten* (from the East)—the *Ossies,* as they would later call us for years.

As I reentered the air-raid shelter, I figured I would have to find a new place to build my nest. I could not have left my coat behind to keep my place, because when people are hungry and desperate and unbelievably poor, honesty and decency somehow leave their consciousness for a while, to return only when things are better again.

When I finally found my old place, the soldier next to me had put his canteen in my spot. He let me take a drink from it, and I gratefully handed it back to him. Nobody was saying a word; we were all alone with our fears and our sorrows and maybe just a glimmer of hope.

It was eerily quiet.

As I was rebuilding my nest, I did not know whether to lie on my coat or cover myself with it. So I chose to lie on it. I knew that I would not be able to sleep a wink because I was much too hungry, worried, and uncomfortable. I put the little suitcase under my head and, actually, with its soft leather, it made quite a good pillow.

People around me were starting to snore softly, but of course, I was not going to sleep, and my mind began to wander to all sorts of thoughts ...

"There is gunfire all around, and we are not sure whether it is the Americans or the Russians."

"Will we actually arrive in Hamburg tomorrow?"

"Will we get something to eat?"

"God, this concrete floor is hard!"

I imagined that I was in my soft bed at home. At home. And then I was asleep.

It is strange. I remember the first day of that trip in every detail, yet the second day is mostly a blur. There was a feeling of being on automatic pilot. You feel nothing. No hunger, no thirst, no pain, no grief, no hope. You just move with the crowd, and you actually feel a certain amount of security and direction if someone tells you to get in line.

What I remember next was standing in a line in a receiving camp in Hamburg, where a British MP was checking our papers. Mine were in a little bag around my neck, along with a few German marks and the note from my mother.

"Do you understand English, or do I have to get an interpreter?" asked the MP.

"I understand English." My old English teacher, Fräulein Ehlers, with the funny bent legs, who was so old that she had even been my mother's teacher, would have been proud of me.

"If you want to stay in Hamburg, you will have to get a residency permit from the military government. You have three days. Hamburg cannot take any more refugees. Do not try to stay illegally."

I said that I had some possible addresses and showed the MP my mother's little paper slip. He wrote something on his list, handed me my papers, and called, "Next!" pointing to the next person in a very long line.

The next queue was for the bathrooms. We were obviously in a German military barracks, and the line was endless. Someone came along and handed us a large tin cup and a spoon and said, "Hold on to this. It is for your food." Then I saw someone coming along the line, pouring water into the tin cups. I felt that I was running out of hands. I put on my heavy coat, although it was August, then put the little suitcase between my feet and held out my tin cup just in time. I drank the water dutifully, just because everyone else was drinking theirs. I did not even know that I was thirsty or should be. I don't like water. Never have, never will.

The next thing I remember is that I was sitting on the top bunk of a triple-tiered bunk bed, watching my roommates. They were not the ones I had worked with in Schwerin, and they were a chirpy, busy, and efficient lot. The unlimited amount of hot and very good potato soup we had received in our tin cups seemed to have given them new energy. They were making up their beds, combing each other's hair, packing and repacking their rucksacks, counting their money by spreading their bank notes and coins on their beds, and chatting endlessly.

Their main concern was, as it should be, to find transportation quickly to wherever there might be someone to stay within the British Zone, or to try and find a job. We were all under the auspices of the Red Cross, and my roommates were hoping that there might be some help from there.

Suddenly, someone noticed me, high up on my third-level bunk.

"Hey, *Kleinchen*" (little one), "where are you going tomorrow?"

"I have the address of a neighbor who lives in Blankenese," I answered and did not let them know that I did not really have an address.

"Ooh!" came a chorus in unison. I did not know at the time that Blankenese was one of the most elite addresses in Hamburg.

"Do you have any money?" came the next question.

"Not very much. I have not really thought about it," was my stupid but honest answer.

"What are you going to do? Are you going to get a residency permit, and are you at least trying to get a job?"

"Yes, I am sure that I can get a residency permit. No, I won't get a job. I have to try and find a school to continue my education until I can get a visa to go to England and live with my father." Again, not a good answer. Except for a few "Oohs," I was greeted by stony silence.

That's when I knew that I was different, that I had been raised in a different world, and that this was definitely not the time to open my little suitcase. I curled up, still wearing that now rather grimy nurse's dress, covered myself with my coat, and slipped the little suitcase under my head. I felt more alone than I had ever felt in my life.

The next morning, as I was once more in a long line to report and get breakfast, I heard my name being called, and a Tommy came up to me and wordlessly handed me a slip of paper. It was the address of Mr. and Mrs. Schnoor, who lived in Langenhorn.

Bless the German bureaucracy. They register everybody and everything; the German system had quickly been adopted by the equally well-organized British military government. The Schnoors had stayed at our house temporarily after they were bombed out in Hamburg in the summer of 1943. My mother had found them a room in a village, and they returned to Hamburg sometime later in the war.

The following day, I was able to leave the receiving camp with strict instructions to report to the military housing agency within three days. I knew Hamburg well enough to find the nearest *S-Bahn* (streetcar) station. I had heard that the British had the public transportation system running within a few days of their occupation. I bought a ticket to Langenhorn and got on the train as if nothing had happened.

When I looked out of the window, I thought my heart would stand still. I saw only miles and miles of rubble. No buildings, no trees, no traffic.

My mother had been to the outskirts of Hamburg after the fire bombings to help the injured. She brought as many as she could to Schwerin to treat them and to find housing for them. We heard often enough that over forty thousand were killed in the air raid of July 1943 and more than one million people were homeless. Yet the amount of devastation in Hamm and Harburg, the industrial and working class areas of Hamburg, was simply unimaginable. There had never been any pictures in the newspapers or in the weekly news films shown regularly in the movie houses.

The view from the window got better as we made our way further north. After I got off at the station at Langenhorn, I saw nothing but gardens with small garden huts. Gardening was a popular hobby, and in better times many people from Hamburg had such a garden on the outskirts of town. But now this was where people lived, and the garden paths had names, and the huts had numbers.

I walked and walked, and finally I found the Schnoors, who lived in a small, one-room hut in the middle of a vegetable garden. I did not even remember the Schnoors, because there had been so many people at our house during the past three years; but both of them remembered me, and both of them cried when they saw me. I must have been quite a sight in that dirty dress, unwashed and incredibly sad and tired.

Grandma Schnoor hugged and hugged me and said, "Your

mother took care of us, and now we will take care of you."

They put a blanket and a pillow on the floor for me to sleep on, and they shared their potato soup and their weekly ration of 200 grams (6 ounces) of ground horseflesh with me. Their love and their kindness restored me.

Looking for Tula

For the next two days I stayed with the Schnoors.

Grandma Schnoor took my dress and underwear and washed everything in a small tin bowl. While my clothes were hanging outside drying in the August sunshine, she gave me the same tin bowl so that I could take a sponge bath and wash my hair. That was the only bowl she had, and we used it for everything. She even found an old comb with a few teeth missing and a well-used toothbrush; those things became my very own for a whole year. There was no toothpaste, but when you have not brushed your teeth for almost a week, salt works wonders.

While my clothes were drying, I wore Grandma Schnoor's nightgown, and Grandpa Schnoor led me around his vegetable garden. A neighbor had given him some seeds in the spring and, while there was fighting and dying all around, those vegetables had grown as if they knew that they would save people's lives later in the year.

After the dress dried, Grandma Schnoor borrowed an electric iron from a neighbor, and within three hours she presented me with a respectable outfit. The pinstripe dress was made like a sack, straight up and down, and Grandma Schnoor simply cut the straps from my now useless apron and made a belt. After Grandpa Schnoor used one of the safety pins from the apron to pin a flower on my shoulder, Grandma Schnoor and I were ready to walk into the village to buy groceries.

At that time the German population was allotted 770 calories a day, mostly made up of bread and potatoes, and until I could get food stamps, the Schnoors shared their rations with me. We stood in line for a long time—first at the grocery shop to get two eggs, a tiny bit of cheese, and a few grams of flour, then at the butcher's, for two hundred grams of ground horseflesh. Thank goodness for that wonderful vegetable garden. We cooked the meat with some cabbage and potatoes, and the horseflesh was not bad at all and went quite long way.

After two days of the Schnoors' spoiling and loving care, I was ready for the world. That meant that I would have to face the housing authorities and the residence registration offices in Hamburg, and I was advised to go there early in the morning to get in line long before the offices were open. Grandma Schnoor gave me some change for the S-Bahn and the *U-Bahn* (underground train) and an apple for the road. Oh, yes, we lived in the lap of luxury in Langenhorn.

There was a list of all the important offices and their locations at every subway station, and I soon found my way around Hamburg. My first stop was the office to get my *Aufenthaltsgenehmigung*, my residency permit.

The office was in one of those huge buildings along the Alster, the river that flows through Hamburg, and in the center of town it is as wide and calm as a big lake.

The warnings were correct. Although it was still before 8:00 a.m., the line at the office for residency permits went halfway around the block. By the time I got inside about two hours later and actually got to talk to somebody, I had heard the life story of everyone around me. I produced my military discharge document and the little scrap of paper from my mother with my father's address in England.

The Tommy behind the desk noted my father's information and said, "We'll see what we can do about England, but for the local addresses you have to contact the housing authority near the *Rathaus*" (City Hall). "I'll extend your residency permit by one week, which means you'll receive a food rationing ticket for seven days. Come back in one week, and if you have found your friends or relatives, we'll talk about an extension of your permit. If you have not found a place to stay by that time, you will have to leave Hamburg within forty-eight hours."

When I timidly asked where I would go, he raised an eyebrow and said, "Back to where you came from, I suppose."

I knew I had to locate Tula Heinemann, because I would never get a permit to stay with the Schnoors in their one-room garden hut.

The military housing authority was near the Rathaus, that magnificent building from the glorious times in the middle ages when Hamburg was one of the leading cities in the Hanseatic

League. The Rathaus was practically undamaged during the air raids and the battle of Hamburg at the end of the war; I had well over an hour to study the beautiful façade as I joined the queue for the housing offices.

I felt optimistic. If this office had found the Schnoors in their garden hut so quickly, they surely would find Tula who, according to some neighbors, lived in a real apartment in Blankenese, a suburb of Hamburg that survived the bombing intact.

My disappointment must have shown on my face. In fact, I had to hold on to the desk as the German civil servant said to me, after an extensive search of the handwritten entries in several huge registration books that had miraculously survived the bombing, "There is no Tula Heinemann living anywhere in Hamburg that I can see." When he saw how terribly disappointed I was, he added kindly, "Come back the day after tomorrow. I'll have someone else go through those books one more time."

I was stunned and could not believe that there was no record of Tula Heinemann at all. The authorities would never permit me to stay at the Schnoors' hut. It had no indoor plumbing, no space for an extra bed. The only reason the Schnoors were permitted to stay where they were was because they were duly registered residents of Hamburg and had lost their home in a bombing raid. I sat on a bench overlooking the Alster, ate my precious apple, and got back on the train to the Schnoors'.

I can't remember at all what I did during the next two days. I hope that I helped Grandma Schnoor with the laundry or the endless vegetable peeling, or Grandpa Schnoor in the garden, but that was not likely, since I did not have a clue how to do any of those things.

Two days later, I was once more on my way to the housing authority near the Rathaus, with change for the train and an apple for my midday meal in my pocket.

This time the line was just as long—maybe longer—and I was not at all hopeful as I approached the man who had helped me before. He recognized me, got up and shook my hand. That's the German way of greeting people, but that courtesy is not usually extended to people in line at the housing authority. Apparently, there had been a communication from the office of residency permits, asking to be of special help to me. Because the International Red Cross had been requested to find my father in England, I was entitled to stay in Hamburg until the contact was made.

"I may have something for you," said the man behind the desk. "Although there is no record of any Tula Heinemann, we found a Wolfgang Heinemann, who is registered and living with his sister Gertrud Fischer in Hochkamp near Blankenese."

I jumped up with excitement and said, "That's Wölfi. I know Wölfi. He was always away at the university, studying law. Yes, Tula's real name is Gertrud, only nobody ever calls her that, and she did marry a captain by the name of something at the beginning of the war."

The man was smiling as he handed me a slip of paper with Tula's real name and her address and said, "Now, we have no way of getting in touch with your friend. Go and see her, and if you can stay with her, report to the office of residency permits at once. Good luck!"

I was out of there like a flash, running all the way to the Dammtor station, and after arriving in Langenhorn, I ran all the way to the Schnoors to bring them the good news.

The next morning, I took my winter coat and my still-not-opened little suitcase and left early. My goodbye to those wonderful people was short. I loved them for what they had done for me, but we all knew that our time together was limited.

At the station, I found out that Hochkamp was just one station before Blankenese. I got my ticket and followed the map of the S-Bahn route on the ceiling of the carriage, so I knew exactly when the Hochkamp stop would come and when I had to get off. I had to ask my way to my destination, and I can't remember the street name anymore, except that it was a very long walk.

The place turned out to be a typical German apartment building with three stories and six apartments, a basement, and a loft. There was a small garden in front and a big lawn with a swing and many clotheslines in the back.

I rang the bell to apartment B, and a few minutes later Tula stood in the door. We had not met in about ten years, and we had both changed a lot, but we recognized each other. She did not exactly greet me with open arms. How could she? People were escaping from the Soviet Zone all the time, and they all rang the doorbells of those who had moved to places in the West and established themselves before the horrors of Soviet occupation took over Pomerania, Mecklenburg, and Brandenburg.

Tula just looked at me and said, "Come in. Are you hungry?"

I shook my head and asked, "Can I stay here for a few days?" When she nodded, I said, "I just need to wash my face and then have a few moments to myself."

Tula looked at me with my heavy coat and my little suitcase, and if she thought that I was small and pathetic she certainly did not show it. "We have no hot water and at the moment no gas to heat a kettle. But there is soap and a towel. After that you can go to my bedroom and unpack. See you later."

As I sat on Tula's big bed and I opened my little suitcase and saw that the upper layer consisted of large, tightly wrapped bandages and many screw-capped ointment containers. I slowly unwrapped the bandages, and money fell out; a lot of money! I unwrapped all of the bandages, and more and more money fell out.

I rewound every bandage carefully, since no first aid trainee would ever leave an unwrapped bandage around, then I began to tackle the ointment containers. Every one of those containers had a thin layer of ointment on top, then a layer of parchment paper, then a big roll of small-denomination German bank notes. I saw that the lower layer of the suitcase held my heavyweight blue winter dress, quite a bit of underwear, and some stockings. I looked at my treasures in amazement.

My mother must have worked all night to pack this suitcase,

after working for years to amass this much cash. She knew that it would take quite a while before I would get a visa for England and that I had left home without any visible means of support and gone to stay in Hamburg, a war-torn, overcrowded, and starving city.

I carefully counted the money and then recounted it. There were an amazing forty-five thousand Reichsmark. Enough to buy a large house or several cars, or to travel around the world more than once! But there were no houses to buy. In fact, there was nothing to buy; the stores were totally empty, and who would want to go traveling?

But there was the black market, where one could buy things to barter. I would have money to go to school, help with what little there was in household expenses, and pay for my voyage to England, if it should ever come to that.

After I repacked the contents of my suitcase, I went into the kitchen to speak to Tula. The gas had come on, and she was cooking something for her two-year-old daughter, Margaret. Without looking up, she said, "I don't have any more beds, but we can roll up a towel and put it over the joint between my two beds. You'll have Cohn on one side" (she was an East Prussian refugee) "and me on the other. We are eight people in this apartment, but you are welcome to stay as long as you need."

It is important to note that Tula offered me shelter long before she knew that I had English connections and thereby connections to the military government, and that I also had a lot of cash. The terrible war, and the difficult time after the defeat, brought out the very best and the very worst in people. When I later on saw, heard, and learned about all the horrible wrongs that the Germans had committed, I was comforted by the thought that there were a lot of good and decent Germans too.

How lucky I was!

Living in Tula's House

My first morning at Tula's, I got up early without disturbing Tula or Margaret and went to the office of residency permits. It worried me that I did not have a permit to stay in Hamburg and that my food stamps had run out.

I got to my destination one hour before they opened, but at least the line was not around the block yet. When it was finally my turn, I explained that I had found some friends with a three-room apartment with only seven residents, and that they were willing to take me in until I made contact with my father in England.

The man behind the desk was a German, and I still had to get used to the effect it had on German people when they heard that I had connections in England. I immediately was treated with courtesy and consideration. If they had only known how tenuous those connections really were and how little I was able to do for them, or even for myself for that matter. My residency permit was extended, I can't remember for how long, and I even got the appropriate food ration stamps.

My next destination was in Langenhorn at the Schnoors in their little garden hut. I had made a tight roll of several one hundred mark bills, which I slipped into Grandma Schnoor's hand. She started to cry and assured me that they did not want to be paid for what they had done for me.

I am sure they did not think of money when they took me in, and they got a small pension from the efficient British administration, but the thought of being able to buy a few ounces of butter on the black market, or even half a pound of coffee, the greatest luxury of all to the Germans, must have been a great comfort.

Grandma Schnoor asked, "Have you eaten?"

For the first time in my life, I gave the reply that would be my standard answer for the next year after the feeling of hunger had become a habit, "I don't remember."

She called Grandpa Schnoor in, and we sat together, drinking Grandma Schnoor's wonderful mint tea from the garden and eating a little piece of bread with cottage cheese.

After leaving the Schnoors and feeling rich and secure with a residency permit and food ration stamps, I went back to Tula's house and finally was relaxed enough to look around and meet the people with whom, as it turned out, I would spend the next year.

I still can't grasp the incredible kindness of Tula, whom I barely remembered from my childhood days, for taking me in. I knew Tula and the family Heinemann from the early thirties. They lived across the street when I lived with my grandmother. There were three girls and one boy who were at least ten years older than me; Tula was the oldest. There also was a little girl my age, who was born much too late to a too-old mother and had a congenital kidney defect.

Irmgard, or Irmchen as I called her, was an invalid from birth and was in and out of the hospital. When Irmchen was at home, her mother would come and ask my grandmother if I could come over and play with her.

Irmchen was far too ill to play, but I would sit by her bed and read to her, or I would draw funny people for her or, best of all, I would show her the newest ballet steps I had just learned.

I remember Irmchen to this day. She died when she was nine years old, and it is possible that Tula remembered this when I arrived at her front door.

Tula's house, as I called it, was a three-room apartment with a small kitchen and a bathroom, and I don't think the whole place was larger than about one thousand square feet. There were eight of us living there for the entire year I was in Hamburg.

First, there was Tula, in her early thirties, and her two-year-old daughter, Margaret. Tula's husband was an army captain who was missing on the Russian front. She was never notified that he was a Russian prisoner of war. I was told years later that one day about four years after the war ended, he just appeared in her doorway and broke down crying. He was a sick and broken man, but he did come home.

Next came Cohn, who was a stout, rather rough-mannered East

Prussian woman in her twenties, who looked old for her age. Cohn was chief cook in a military hospital/POW camp, and although we shared a bed for a whole year, I don't think I ever knew her first name. Tula, Cohn, and I shared Tula's marital bed; I was in the middle on the hard part where the two beds were pushed together, the way the Germans do it. There was hardly room in that bedroom for Margaret's tiny cot, and we had to move it every time we wanted to get to the closet.

Then there was Tula's sister, Polly—I have no idea what her real name was—and her husband, Karl. He wore his hat at a rakish angle, had terrible skin and bedroom eyes that looked in opposite directions, and was a chain-smoker—*but* Karl had connections in the black market, and it is largely due to his activities that we survived at all. To his credit, Karl never asked to be called Charley. Polly and Karl had a son who was about twelve years old and hardly ever came out of the one room they shared. I saw him once in a while when he came through the apartment on his way to school, carrying his books in a string bag.

Tula's brother, Wolfgang, lived with us too. I remembered him as Wölfi from ten years earlier. He did not do anything as far as I could see. He was, or had been, a law student, and I can remember his little sister telling me years before, "Wolfgang has flunked his exam *again.*" He was a sensible man, and I considered him an *almost lawyer,* and therefore I discussed my money with him.

I followed his advice and deposited thirty thousand Reichsmark in the Deutsche Bank.

That was good advice, because with Karl's dealings in the black market our house could have been raided at any time, and my money would have been gone. I could safely leave the money in the bank when I left for England, where it would be useless to me anyway. When the Reichsmark was finally devalued in 1950, I got 4 percent in the new Deutsche Mark.

Wolfgang became a friend and I trusted him completely, but he did not want me to call him Wölfi anymore. He came along on the many trips I had to make to the housing authority when I tried to extend my residency permit. Those trips could be very depressing. Large parts of Hamburg were totally bombed out, and the town was crawling with refugees, former concentration camp inmates, and German ex-soldiers, all struggling for food and shelter.

Wolfgang did get me the permit. He must have told them a tall story about my famous father who was a professor at the University of Cambridge (not true!) and my 50 percent British citizenship (not true either). He talked a lot about that 50 percent British citizenship. It must have made him feel good, and they went for it! Within a week, I was a legal resident of Hamburg entitled to food stamps for as long as I needed.

There was one more man in our group. Nice guy, always smiling and gentle. He played with Margaret, was friendly and helpful, but never went out. I have no idea where he slept. Certainly not in our bed, and in retrospect I think he was in hiding. He did not strike me as an SS man or even an arch-Nazi. I was pretty sensitive to the signs, but I never asked. Nobody asked questions, and no one was looking for trouble. Those were incredible times!

I don't remember the kitchen too well, because I think that was pretty much Tula's domain. She did the cooking and planning and food distribution. She was very fair, and if we got only sliced, raw turnips for several meals in a row, then that was all there was, and people groaned but never complained and certainly did not blame Tula. She probably had a little talk with Cohn once in a while when things got really bad for too long a time. Cohn had much better connections than any of us.

We never ate together as a group. Maybe it was because there was no space for a large table, and maybe there were just not enough plates and knives and forks to go around. Polly took her and Karl's share of food to their room; Wolfgang and the Mystery Man ate in the living room; Cohn ate at work; and Tula, little Margaret, and I ate in the kitchen. There was so little food and everybody left the table hungry, so we made as little fuss about mealtime as possible. I don't ever remember doing the dishes, and that was a good thing. People did not think of me as much of a housekeeper, and how right they were.

The bathroom was another matter. I remember every inch of that place. The bathtub was used as a storage place, and it also held individual boxes of dirty laundry. If we had ever had a chance to take a shower or a bath, I am sure we would have gladly cleaned out the tub, but in that entire year the only hot water we had came from the kettle in the kitchen—that is, if we had gas. Once in a while, Karl got a piece of soap on the black market, and we all shared it and treated it as a real treasure. I think my phobia about wet, dissolving soap in a soap dish must stem from that time in my life. I know I have driven people crazy with that over the years, both at home and especially in the lab where I worked as an adult.

If I remember correctly, three or four times during that year Karl actually brought home a roll of toilet paper, which was greeted with great joy. There was almost a ceremony as I put it on the usually empty toilet paper holder. The rest of the time we used newspaper, but even that was often in short supply, and I remember being told that I was cutting the pieces too small.

Newspaper was also the only thing we had for our feminine sanitary needs, and that remains one of my worst memories of that year in Hamburg. To this day, my heart goes out to all of those women in refugee camps or in other situations where even a newspaper is not an option.

Since we were all refugees, we did not bring any towels or bed sheets to Tula's house. All of us had to use her sheets and towels, and since she had been a war bride, she did not have much linen. I put myself in charge of towels and linen—actually the entire bathroom. There were two towels a week, one for the men and one for the women. I made a great fuss over getting them dried out during the day for use the next morning, and I am still fussy about that.

Once a month we could do laundry, but only if Karl had been able to procure laundry soap and some firewood from the black market. The wood was needed so that we could heat the water in a cauldron, which was in that part of the basement called the *Waschküche,* the laundry room. Fortunately, I did not have much to do with what actually happened in the Waschküche;

Polly took care of that, but it was my responsibility to hang up the laundry in the backyard, take it down, fold it, and put it away. That was a hard task when it was raining, and it rained a lot. I had to try and dry things in the basement and all over the apartment, but I loved that job when the weather was fine. It was the best exercise I got all that year.

I realize that I have said nothing about interpersonal relationships, and as much as I try to think about it, I really think that there weren't any. I don't ever remember a few of us sitting together and laughing or playing cards or even crying on each others' shoulders. Tula never cried about not being able to feed her child or whether she would ever see her husband again. None of us knew a single thing about Cohn, who obviously had lost everything she ever owned and everyone she ever loved. Wolfgang had a wife and a child in the Russian Zone, but he never talked about them.

We were existing together, surviving together, and every one of us knew that we could not do it alone. I was grateful to all of them, but there were no emotional ties whatsoever. I remember that time as being always alone, an outsider with a dream.

Often, when I was not too weak from hunger, I walked along the banks of the River Elbe, especially when cargo ships passed again and again, and I tried to imagine what it was like at their destinations. With hunger and chronic fatigue as my constant state of existence, my body forgot that it had been like a well-trained instrument with at least three ballet lessons a week for many years.

Yes, when I think of that year in Hamburg, it is the hunger that I remember most.

My British Connection

Shortly after I got my residency permit in Hamburg, I went to one of the most elegant hotels on the Alster: the *Vier Jahreszeiten* (Four Seasons), which housed the British military government.

I walked up and down the sweeping staircases, along a seemingly endless number of red-carpeted corridors, and into many ornate rooms until I found the office that housed the Swiss Red Cross.

I remember feeling incredibly shabby and badly groomed, but the uniformed official behind the desk was courteous, and I lodged my appeal to find and contact my father in England.

The only address I had was Papworth Hall, Cambridge, England, and that was from long before the war. I did not know his birth date or recent address. All I knew was that his name was Otto Marienfeld and that he had been at Papworth Hall in 1936.

The Red Cross man took it all down, what there was of it, and said that I would be contacted if there was any news. Frankly, I did not have much hope, because the German infrastructure was so broken that I just could not imagine that there were other parts of Europe that were actually functioning.

If anything was working at all, it was certainly the Swiss Red Cross, because after about two weeks I got a letter, hand delivered by a British MP, which of course made the neighborhood gasp. The message stated that I was to present myself personally to Colonel Swanson, Chief Medical Officer of Health for the City of Hamburg, within forty-eight hours at the Hotel Vier Jahreszeiten, Alster Ufer, Hamburg—all in one sentence, the German way.

I thought my heart would stop as I read it aloud to anyone who happened to be present in the living room. Everybody started to talk at once; Wolfgang offered to come along.

I just said, "This is something I must do alone," and put on my hat—yes, I wore a hat in those days; everybody in Hamburg wore a hat, even if they had to get it on the black market like me—and I was out the door.

My special-delivery letter gained me access to the Vier Jahreszeiten, which I remembered from my visit to the Swiss Red Cross, and within minutes I was ushered into the office of Colonel Swanson. My entrance was accompanied by several "Yes, sirs" and "No, sirs" and military salutes, which made me feel rather special.

The little man behind the desk had thinning red hair and a big red mustache, and he did not rise. He asked me in a rather quiet, hesitant voice and excellent German, "Do you know why you are here?" To which I sort of shrugged my shoulders. I never did catch on to that "Yes, sir," "No, sir" bit.

He continued, "I am an old friend of your father's. We met at the University of Edinburgh, and I have a letter from him to you. Read it at home. Is there anything I can do for you right now? Are you getting enough to eat?"

My answer to that question came quickly, "No, not really. We are always hungry, but we are getting by."

"We are tightly rationed, too, and I can't give any food away, but you can come and have dinner with me. Would you like that?"

Of course I said, "Yes." But a little red flag went up, and a few of my mother's warnings shot through my head.

When I got home I read my father's letter. It was very short. He told me that he had remarried (a nurse) and was Public Health Officer for Tuberculosis in South Shields, County Durham, a small industrial town in the northeast of England near Newcastle upon Tyne. He told me that he had met Colonel Swanson while he was at the University of Edinburgh and that Colonel Swanson had agreed to transmit letters between us and assist me if he could.

The next evening I had dinner with Colonel Swanson. I felt like a queen as I was ushered into an elegant private dining room. The table was set for two, with flowers and wineglasses, and I really felt dowdy in that eternal blue schoolgirl dress. But thanks to my rigorous upbringing, there was nothing schoolgirl about my table manners or my conversation. In fact, I was probably a lot more sophisticated than my middle-aged British host.

The meal was delicious, and I really had to control myself not to gobble. But after dinner I learned that my mother was right and realized the truth behind the adage, "A man wants only one thing." The good colonel took his glass, went over to a big armchair, and sat down. As I walked over to the other chair, he gently pulled me onto his lap. There I sat, wineglass in hand, and while looking him straight in the eye, I said, "I don't do that sort of thing."

His reply was, "Most women do, but maybe you are not a woman yet."

The answer to that one was easy. I replied, "That's right," and sat in the other chair.

Whether I *did that sort of thing* or not, I certainly would not do it with a man who was my father's age and who had the nerve to think he could buy me with a dinner!

The colonel asked me not to mention this to my father, who would be angry. I gave him that promise, and I kept it.

Colonel Swanson was incredibly helpful to me during the next several, difficult months. He got me enrolled in the School of Languages, where I studied for, and received, my interpreter's certificate. He was the intermediary for the correspondence between my father and me.

He saw to it, on my father's request, that I got a weekly copy of the *Manchester Guardian,* which was of great to help develop my English—and great for the bathroom. And in late July 1946, almost one year later, he was the one who handed me my military exit permit, the very first to be issued by the military government in the British Zone of Germany.

However, he never invited me to dinner again.

A Winter of Learning

Thanks to Colonel Swanson and, therefore, with the blessing of the military government and the appropriate paperwork, I was able to enroll in the School of Languages the very next day, and I was thrilled about that.

The public schools in the British Zone had reopened in September of 1945, but I could not get permission to attend because of my refugee status. Only present and returning residents of Hamburg were admitted. The schools were overcrowded, because so many buildings had been destroyed. There was no shortage of teachers, because everybody who could possibly get out of the Russian Zone had come into the British and American Zones.

Rather than just sit in Tula's house or, worse yet, become an active participant in the housekeeping, I would have had to try to volunteer in one of the military hospitals. Even that was difficult, because there was no shortage of labor in the British Zone in spite of the critical food and housing situation.

The School of Languages was a wonderful solution for me. Established by the military government, it was located in one of the large villas that they had commandeered. We had classes every day, and it was a long way from Blankenese to Uhlenhorst on the other side of the Alster.

I was gone practically all day.

Karl managed to get a pencil and some notepaper on the black market. Don't worry, I paid him for everything, and I found that I was so much better off than my classmates. There were no books of any kind, and the only thing we had were the notes we took while the kindly lady who was our English teacher talked on and on. Without paper and pencil you had to keep it all in your head.

Mrs. Winter was an Englishwoman from Bristol, the widow of a German man who had been killed early in the war. She was really a tragic figure, left alone in wartime Germany where English people were not popular, especially during air raids in air-raid shelters, and she had to wait until the British government was ready to repatriate her.

Once a week, I went to Colonel Swanson's office and picked up my copy of the *Manchester Guardian*. I read that paper word for word from beginning to end. Often, I would take it with me on the long train ride into Hamburg, and I would always have some information to share with the news-hungry Germans looking over my shoulder.

Mrs. Winter and the students in class all shared my treasure, and although the lying and the Nazi propaganda had stopped, the news in the *Manchester Guardian* was still quite different from what we heard on the radio. Sometimes I would let Mrs. Winter take a copy home over the weekend, but she always returned it, knowing full well that that precious paper still had another purpose.

Occasionally, our whole class was allowed to attend something like the *Nuremberg Trials,* which went on in all major cities in the British and American Zones. While we did not get to see the major criminals, who were all tried in Nuremberg, we sat through the trials of some very unsavory characters—those who had been the guards in the concentration camps and committed other gruesome crimes. It was a devastating experience for many of the students who, unlike me, had been kept completely in the dark about the war crimes. Since I had known about the horror for a long time, I was not distracted by the facts but was able to follow the actual language part of the hearings, and I did the translations in my head.

All of the accused were Germans, and the official interpreters were all British, and since my English was pretty good by this time, I thought that sometimes the interpretations left much to be desired.

I talked to Mrs. Winter about that and asked her why she was not an official interpreter; I knew that her German was so much better than that of the official interpreters.

Mrs. Winter explained that she had to give up her British citizenship when she married her German husband while living under the Nazis, and she had been a translator for them on many occasions. Now, under the British regime, she was forbidden to do verbal interpreting and was permitted to do only written translations. What a loss during that critical time.

Mrs. Winter just laughed and said that she considered herself lucky that she did not land in a concentration camp like so many British nationals at the end of the war and that she was not interned by the British for having given up her British citizenship and cooperating with the Germans. She was so nice and helpful to us, but by her own admission, she had been skating on thin ice.

My love for the English language, which has never left me, was stimulated by my constant contact with that language. An interest in Britain and in America came quite naturally with that knowledge.

Imagine my delight when Karl came home one day with a copy of Margaret Mitchell's book, *Gone with the Wind*. Although it was in German, I loved reading about Americans and their way of life. I did not realize at the time that the era of *Gone with the Wind* had long since passed.

I read the book whenever I could, but after my studying in the evening and the chronic fatigue brought on by starvation, I usually went to bed early.

Unfortunately—or maybe fortunately—I was only halfway through the book when the call came that my exit visa had arrived, and I had to leave the book in Germany. Shortly after my arrival in England I had my twentieth birthday, and my father gave me a beautifully bound copy of *Gone with the Wind* in English! I have often said that Scarlet O'Hara had a lot to do with my love for the English language.

My constant hunger during that year was often quite unbearable, and when I really could not stand it anymore, I would drag myself to the back door of Cohn's hospital kitchen, and she would give me some soup or some cabbage. I would sit there like a beggar on the back steps and gobble the food. My room- and bedmate, of whom I knew so little, would say, "Poor baby, you are not used to the tough times yet, are you?"

Sometimes Cohn would bring home a big pot of a mishmash of vegetables and potatoes and maybe a tiny bit of meat. I suspect that she scraped it from the bottom of her huge cooking pots prior to washing them, and I am not at all sure whether she did not scrape the plates of the patients as well, but all of us were past caring. Tula carefully dished out the food so that we all got an equal share, and we were so grateful for every scrap that Cohn brought home to us.

In March 1946, my cousin Dorli arrived at our doorstep. She had crossed the border from the Russian Zone illegally and secretly during the night and was in search of her father. He had been a big Nazi doctor and was now interned somewhere in the British Zone, awaiting trial. She was trying to find him and bring him news of her mother and her four siblings, who had all survived and were getting on as well as anyone could in the Soviet Zone.

Best of all, she brought me a letter from my mother. It was the first time I had heard from her in eight months, and I was over- joyed to learn that she was alive. The Russians commandeered her house shortly after I left, and she took a room in the house of one of her patients. She continued her medical practice as best she could in that one room.

Dorli promised me that she would get word to my mother that I was all right and still waiting for my military exit permit. She stayed for only one night, and I let her have my spot between Tula and Cohn. At least it was a bed with a pillow and a share of a blanket. I slept on the floor, with my dress rolled up as a pillow, covered by my winter coat.

Those were strange times, which in some mysterious way brought out the best in us. The spirit of community and equality, and the fact that I had been so readily accepted, was a gift and a valuable experience for me.

A Matter of Survival

After I had spent two or three weeks in Tula's house, Karl approached me and asked whether I had ever set up and operated a still. My answer was, "Of course I have. How else would I have got all those As in science?"

Karl enlisted my talents as a high school chemist and put me in charge of a distillery, which he was planning to operate at night in the basement.

Setting up that still was no great trick, since he provided all the parts, obviously lifted from some surviving high school laboratory. He also provided the mash—some disgusting stuff made from rotten potato peelings and I would rather not know what else—and the empty bottles, the corks, and the caraway seeds. He prepared the mash in buckets, which he got from Cohn, and you just never asked her any questions. I assume, but I am not sure, that most of the potato peelings came from Cohn too. The mash had to be tended carefully, stirred at regular intervals, and he seemed to know exactly when it was ready for me.

I can't remember what our source of heat was, because we were without gas and electricity for long periods of time, and I have to assume that Karl provided something dangerous in cylinders.

I had to stay awake during my distilling duties, which naturally were always during the night.

It was no easy task with an empty stomach, but I always felt that it was for a good cause for our community, and that thought kept me going. I produced the best *Kümmel* (Schnapps) this side of the river Elbe and was proud of it.

Karl went to do "his business" in the St. Pauli district of Hamburg, which was the area around the harbor with lots of bars, night clubs, dark little restaurants and, no doubt, houses of prostitution.

I never went down there with him, and I appreciated the fact that he treated me strictly as the cook and not as a business partner in his black market dealings.

In St. Pauli, Karl bartered my Kümmel for bread and milk and occasionally some cheese, laundry soap, toilet paper, or whatever was available. When he came home with his full briefcase, we all gathered around and watched him unpack. Here, too, the eight of us shared every crumb. Although we never talked about my nighttime activities in the basement, I could sense that my standing in the family community had risen quickly and considerably. I could never reach the heights of Karl or Cohn, but I, too, had become a valuable, contributing member.

Shame on me, but I often suspected that Karl lined his own

pockets, because I could not believe that a fifth of my wonderful Kümmel would be worth only one lousy, soggy loaf of bread or box of laundry soap or bottle of milk. It took so many hours in the basement to produce that Kümmel. In retrospect, I was probably quite unfair, and I am glad that I never opened my mouth.

Karl must have had expenses. After all, those rotten potatoes peelings had to have come from somewhere, and so did the bottles, the corks, and the caraway seeds.

When my memories and my loneliness became overwhelming, I took the S-Bahn downtown just as I had done in those years when things were normal and when I was excited to be in the big city. Now it was strange to walk through Hamburg's elegant department stores like the *Alsterhaus* and see the empty shelves. I often went in just to remind myself of the good old days, when you could buy things in Hamburg we never would have been able to buy in provincial little Schwerin.

To keep the doors open, the Alsterhaus sold theater tickets. Yes, in this devastated town you could go to the opera, see plays, and attend ballet performances. The seats were not cheap, but we assumed that the costumes and most of the food for the performers must have come from the black market; nobody could sing a Wagnerian aria or dance on their toes for hours on 770 calories a day. I was a lucky girl to have enough money to attend many wonderful performances during that year.

Some people did some pretty bad things in their desperation. We read in the newspaper that a group of people had taken up the railroad tracks just to the north of Hamburg and were using the wooden ties for firewood and to barter on the black market for food.

The people from Hamburg always blamed the refugees from the East for the bad deeds, and I feel that the rift between the West and the East—the *Wessies* versus the Ossies—started as early as 1945 and has been with us ever since. I do not know whether the railroad ties were stolen by refugees or local people, but I must confess that I was always uncomfortable when Karl brought home firewood to heat the water for our monthly laundry day. We were all desperately cold and hungry, and desperate people do desperate things. I have never once felt guilty for having been part of the only thing that kept all of us alive, and that was the black market.

We survived that cruel winter of 1945-46 as did most of the people in the British and American Zones, but I heard in later years that death from starvation and exposure took its toll in the French and Russian Zones. Although I was often physically miserable, I never lost sight of the fact that I was so very lucky, because I had hope and the dream that I could leave all of it behind and start a new life in a new country.

Leaving Germany

It was not *what* I knew but *whom* I knew—namely my father and his connections—that got me out of Germany in August 1946. I was the first non-Jewish person to leave the British Zone of Germany after the war.

Colonel Swanson must have pulled some incredible strings with the military government, the British Home Office, and the Swiss Red Cross to get me that incredibly valuable piece of paper, the military exit permit. He was smiling all over when he handed me that precious document. I could have hugged and kissed the man in sheer gratitude—but, remembering that little incident at our first and only dinner, I did not.

Before I got too excited, he said, "Remember that this is only an exit permit. It does not provide transportation. It does not even give you permission to enter Britain. There is no way for a German civilian to get across the Channel unless your father has some very good connections."

Well, my father did have such connections.

The only son of the owner of the Tyne-Tees Steam Shipping

Company in Sunderland had contracted tuberculosis at age fourteen. This was at a time when antibiotics were still a microbiologist's dream and tuberculosis was practically a death sentence in the north of England. There was not enough fresh air and sunshine in that part of the country to effect a cure, and during wartime, travel to Switzerland or even the south coast of England where they had tuberculosis sanitariums was impossible. Yet my father, who was becoming one of the leading chest specialists in County Durham, had brought young Roland through, and Roland's father thought that he owed my father a big favor.

When my father approached him—which was not easy for my father, who did not like to ask favors of anyone—Mr. Pemberton said to him, "I have a cargo ship with lumber leaving Hamburg around August 15, and it will dock in Sunderland. Maritime law does not permit us to take any female passengers except for the captain's wife, because we do not have any stewardess on board. Your daughter will have to stay below deck the entire trip. Also, make sure that she brings her own food. My men are on very short rations, and I would not want them to have to share. Let her know to be ready by August 13. She will be notified."

All of this was related to me by Colonel Swanson and I started to make preparations.

We had no potato peelings for the still, so I set out on my own to get a loaf of bread on the black market. This was my first and only trip to St. Pauli, and Karl had given me good directions. That loaf of bread cost me a fortune, and it was so soggy and heavy I could have used it as a lethal weapon.

Packing was easy since I had no possessions. Everything I owned fit into my little suitcase, except for my loaf of bread, which I carried in a cloth bag. I wore my same old schoolgirl dress. I had dyed it black when the blue totally faded, but the black color came off on my underwear. I readied my wooden shoes—which really hurt and had done considerable damage to my feet—my winter coat, and my hat; then I waited.

The call came, I think, on August 16. Fortunately, Tula had a phone by then, and Colonel Swanson did not have to send his motorcycle MP. I was told to be down by the docks at 6:00 a.m. the next morning.

Wolfgang took me to the dock. I don't remember anything about goodbyes to Tula or the family (I hope I said "thank you") or even boarding the ship. I just remember being in a cabin, holding onto my loaf of bread, and hoping that they would bring me some water and show me where the toilet was. I knew that I was going to be okay for the next three or four days.

As I felt the engines starting, I got on my tiptoes and looked out of the porthole. We chugged slowly through Hamburg Harbor, and I saw cargo ships and the many wharfs, most of them still idle, glide by. I was sorry that my porthole faced west because I would not be able to say goodbye to Blankenese, Wedel, or Glückstadt, which are all along the eastern banks of the river.

The estuary of the Elbe River is very long, some sixty nautical miles, and it took our little cargo ship some four hours to reach the open sea. I had plenty of time to reflect as I looked out of the porthole and watched the flat, green landscape of Lower Saxony recede, but I don't remember being particularly philosophic or even excited.

The ship had just started to roll a little bit when there was a knock at the door. When I opened it ever so slightly, a big, hairy hand appeared, holding a steaming mug of tea. As soon as I had a hold of it, the hand disappeared and the door closed.

I must tell you about tea as it is served in the north of England. The tea is incredibly strong, almost black, and laced with a lot of sugar and cream. If there is no cream—and in postwar England there certainly was no cream—it is served with sugar and Carnation evaporated milk. Never ever do they drink that sissy stuff with lemon and artificial sweetener.

I wrapped my hands around the mug and started to drink. To this day I can still smell and taste my first sip of that tea. It was hot and sweet and creamy, and as I felt it slowly flow across my tongue, down my throat, into my stomach, and from there throughout every inch of my body, I could feel my life and my energy and my youth returning to me. No kidding; I was still young and healthy and optimistic enough to be totally revived by one cup of tea!

From that moment on, my trip on the cargo ship across the quite wild North Sea was a pure delight and one of my greatest adventures.

About an hour after the tea there was another knock at the door, and this time I got to see the sailor who said, "The captain is asking you to join us for dinner." I thought I was not hearing right, but I came out of my cabin in a flash. Naturally, I remember every minute of that meal. There were about eight of us at the table. Six crew, the captain, and me. We had some sort of meat pie—something I had never eaten before and found to be absolutely and totally delicious.

It must be remembered that the English, even the less educated ones, are refined, slow eaters. They balance their food on the back of their forks, even the peas—and there are always peas, the dried, bullet-like variety—while we Germans load our forks and shove the food into our mouths, especially when we are desperately hungry. No wonder I had cleared my plate before the British crew had barely started. The engineer who was sitting on my left picked up my empty plate and passed it around to everyone at the table, and they all put a little bit of their food on it. I almost cried with gratitude; in fact, I am almost crying as I am writing this now. Those sailors were so tightly rationed that they really did not get enough food for themselves, and here they were willing to share with a German girl!

I don't remember much about going back to my cabin and crawling into my bunk. I do remember thinking that it had been a long time since I had a bed all to myself. During the night the ship started to roll and creak, and I wrapped myself tighter into my blanket, thinking, "I hope I don't fall out of bed." But the thought of being seasick never once entered my head. I was not going to give up a single morsel of that precious food.

The next morning when I appeared from my cabin, I was greeted with cheers. I was told that we had had a really bad storm, and a few of the crew had been quite miserable. Nevertheless, during the night they listened at my door to make sure that I was all right. When I told them that I was fine, they grinned from ear to ear and after breakfast, of which I remember little, they asked me to come up on the bridge.

It was exciting on the bridge. It was very windy, and I was glad to have my trusty winter coat, but I loved the idea that you could see as far as the eye can see in every direction. The sea had calmed down, and there were just a few little waves, not even whitecaps. I was fascinated by the stuff that was drifting by—timber and all sorts of debris. We also saw two mines, grim reminders of a war that had affected us all.

After a while, the captain asked if I would like to steer the ship. I said, "Yes, I'd love to," and it certainly looked easy enough. You kept your eye on the compass and made sure that the needle stayed in the same place by jiggling the steering wheel a little bit this way and a little bit that way. Ha! It was not as easy as I thought.

I kept my eye on the compass and knew exactly where the needle was supposed to be, but could I keep it that way or at least anywhere near it? No, certainly not!

When I finally handed over the steering of the ship, the captain had me look out of the back window so that I could see the zig-zaggy wake the ship had left while under my command.

I was really embarrassed, but everyone just laughed. I don't recall being asked to take the helm again.

I spent most of the four-day trip up on the bridge, listening to the radio and practicing my English with the crew. This was not easy, because I knew Oxford English, taught by Germans, while most of the crew, except for the captain and the engineer, talked Geordie, that peculiar Newcastle-Tyneside dialect, which some Englishmen never learn to understand and later took me about two years to master.

On the morning of the fourth day, there was a knock at my door, and somebody yelled, "Land!"

I practically flew up to the bridge.

Slowly, as if cautiously, the British coast, my new homeland, came into view. Again, I don't know or remember what my feelings were. I was not terrifically excited, not the way I would later be every time my plane landed in a new country or on a new continent, and I was not particularly sorry to leave Germany behind. I lived in the moment. I was a survivor and let the past and the future take care of itself.

I saw my father standing on the dock in Sunderland. I had last seen him when I was five and had not seen a picture of him since, but I recognized him right away. He came on board, and I don't recall whether he hugged me or not. In retrospect I doubt it, but I do remember that he said in English, "Welcome to England."

As it turned out, England did not exactly welcome this foreigner with open arms. As Colonel Swanson had told me, I only had a military exit permit—no passport and no visa—and quite frankly, the north of England port authorities did not know what to do with me. Again, my father's remarkable connections saved the day.

As a county employee, my father had almost daily contact with the county government and the councilman, Chuta Eade (I am probably hopelessly misspelling that fine gentleman's name). Mr. Eade had recently received a new appointment, namely that of home secretary, which is nothing less than the British equivalent of our secretary of state. My father had the port authorities put a personal call through to him, and guess what? The answer was, "Let her come into the country and tell her to apply to the Housing Department within three days to get a residency permit." Those were almost exactly the same words I had heard in Hamburg from the British military authorities a year before. The British really knew how to run their empire! They ruled it exactly as they ruled their own country.

After that, it was easy. I shook hands with all the crew and met Mr. Pinkerton, the owner of the Tyne-Tees line, who had permitted me to be a passenger on his ship. (It was a most memorable trip for both the crew and their passenger.) Then my father and I were off in a taxi to South Shields, about nine miles to the north.

What followed is pretty much a blur, but I remember letting out a gasp as a double-decker bus came towards us on a narrow street and on the wrong side of the road. I would have a lot to learn.

Once settled in England a bit, I began to think back on Germany. By the time the German population heard about the concentration camps, the ovens, and what really happened, I am afraid they were so overwhelmed from the war and so incredibly hungry that those piles of emaciated bodies they saw in the papers or on the screen were just another part of the war.

These people had lost their country, their dream of power and glory—in fact, many had lost their God. They had been defeated and humiliated, while I, who had been brought up for twelve years to be out of step, to "walk to a different drummer," so to speak, was liberated and was able to start a new life.

✦

Epilogue

The Soviet administration of our town, Schwerin, forced my mother out of her house in the spring of 1947. She had to leave everything behind except for some items from her medical practice, which she used to open a doctor's office in the store of a local electrician.

All over the Soviet Zone, the Russians forced the Social Democrats to form a common party with the Communists; the *Sozialistische Einheitspartei Deutschlands* (SED), the Socialist Unity Party of Germany and, once more, the old social Democrats and the old Communists were as unpopular and as much in political danger as they had been under the Nazis. The newly formed *Stasi*, the East German secret police, was every bit as ruthless as the Gestapo had been.

My mother continued her underground activities, just as she had done during the Nazi years, by helping people to get out of the Russian Zone, either via Berlin, where they had large refugee camps, or across the *Grüne Grenze*—the green border, as the heavily guarded no-man's-land between East and West was called.

One day in the spring of 1951, her name reached the top of the black list, and one of her old Communist friends appeared at her door and told her that she was about to be arrested. She fled, wearing only her nightgown under her coat and carrying her doctor's bag. Using the same connections she had used for so long, she managed to get to Berlin.

She contacted Willy Brandt, a former member of the Socialist Democratic Party and Socialist Workers Party (and later to become chancellor of West Germany), who had returned to Berlin in 1946. Since her reputation preceded her, she got a position as physician in charge of a refugee camp. She supervised the kitchens, treated the patients, and had quite a knack for sorting the Nazis from all the other refugees. She was able to prevent any Nazi from getting on the British and American supply planes, which flew refugees out of Berlin on their return flights—and that is how my mother eventually got into the British Zone.

The postwar Adenauer administration, which had heard of my mother, found her a position in charge of the *Bremerhavener Kinderheim,* a children's convalescent home and summer camp on the North Sea island of Langeoog. She built a small house on the island and went to work seven days a week on her bicycle since there were, and are, no cars permitted on the island. She officially retired at age seventy but continued to take care of anyone on the island who needed her help.

She died in 1981 at age eighty-three and is buried in a small cemetery in the sand dunes of Langeoog, lovingly remembered by many people whose lives she changed and saved.

✦

Acknowledgments

I want to thank my editor and publisher Ruth Anne (a.k.a. Sam) Uhl, of The Cheerful Word, who got me started and then kept me on the right track with competence and sensitivity.

I want to thank my ever patient husband Syd, who never lost faith in me and my ability to write this book.

I thank our friend Ken Blackwell, who supported my efforts and introduced my book and me to the Hendersonville community.

I am so proud of my grandson Chris Alexakis, who has shown so much interest in my family and this work and designed the meaningful cover of this book.

My special thanks go to Dr. Kathrin Günther, a direct descendant of the Strauss family, who followed the writing of this very personal history with compassion and understanding. She is supporting me in the love for my family and my homeland, Germany.

About the Author

Charlotte Hugues Self easily shares her bright smile, and with compassion and generosity of spirit she shares her belief that each of us can affect positive change in our families, in our communities, and across the world as we listen to one another with love and understanding.

Since her childhood during the Hitler years, she has gone on to live a fulfilling life, sharing her passion for social justice as a writer and public speaker. Charlotte received her master of science degree in immunology and laboratory management from California State University at Long Beach in 1976. She headed the newborn screening program of the California State Health Department for the Los Angeles area until she retired at age seventy-four.

In 1950 Charlotte married an Englishman, Eric Dugdale. She has two children, Eric Hugues Dugdale and Annette Dugdale Alexakis, and two grandsons, James and Chris Alexakis, who are the lights of her life.

Charlotte lives in Hendersonville, North Carolina, with her husband, Sydney Self. At age ninety, she is thankful for such a rich life and can often be heard saying, "If you smile at the world, it might just smile back at you!"

Made in the USA
Columbia, SC
06 July 2020